JESUS IS THE REVELATION

JESUS IS THE REVELATION

SHATTERING LIES, TRADITION, & RELIGION

JOHN G. SMITH II

XULON PRESS

Xulon Press
2301 Lucien Way #415
Maitland, FL 32751
407.339.4217
www.xulonpress.com

© 2021 by John G. Smith II

Cover design edited by Clayton (Bear) Smith
Edited by John G. Smith II and Debra Davis

Unless otherwise indicated, Scripture quotations taken from the King James Version (KJV) – *public domain.*

Paperback ISBN-13: 978-1-6628-1320-7

Hard Cover ISBN-13: 978-1-6628-1321-4
Ebook ISBN-13: 978-1-6628-1322-1

In Loving Memory of Tiffany L. Addicks
And remember, Jesus, Loves You

"In the beginning was the Word, and the Word was with God,
and the Word was God."

John 1:1

TABLE OF CONTENTS

SPECIAL APPRECIATION & THANKS

Jesus Christ, for dying on the cross for me! You chose me, even when I didn't choose you! I would like to dedicate this book to several important people in my life. First, to my mother, *Debra Davis*! You have been a picture of loyalty and honor. Through all of your ups and downs, you've never turned your back on Jesus, your children, your husband, or your friends. You've never turned your back on me! You're a loving wife to an amazing man *(Bob)* who spoils you rotten, and you're the best big sister in the world. *You are the perfect example of the kind of woman I want my daughters to become!* Everyone who has ever come in contact with you always says, *"I just adore Debra!"* You have supported me throughout my entire life, even when I didn't deserve it. You've encouraged me through the worst of times in my life. You're a bright light in a dark world and I love you! To my dad *(John L.)* *I will honor you for teaching me to survive on my own.*

To my 23 year old son, Bear, who is fiercely loyal and has the best heart of any man on the planet. You've taught me compassion, as well as how to treat women. Madison, my 21 year old daughter, who recently fell *madly* in love with Jesus. You are my little mother hen, and an amazing woman with a bright future ahead of you. You are loyal to the bone! I've always known you were destined for greatness. I especially cannot forget my youngest daughter *(Bukie.)* You are a little hidden gem. You are the real thing! You inspire me, you spoil me, and know when to tell me, *"Dad, Shut up."* You are just as loyal as the other two. I love all of you so much!

I am grateful to my good friend, *Mr. John Nixon.* It's your loyalty and friendship that always encourages and uplifts me. You always said that I should write a book.

I would like to thank *"the late" Chuck Missler (founder of Koinonia House)* who is a man of God and a ***"treacher"*** on a global level *(a preacher proclaims the Gospel & a teacher unpacks it!)* Your entire life has been a pinnacle of achievement and dedication in revealing Jesus and it has blessed my ministry! I've never learned more from any other source. Your famous quote is, *"Yes, you can prove the Bible!" It is written specifically by design, and if you come to a passage in the Bible and it seems difficult, then rejoice, because **there** lies a discovery!" Mr. Missler* went to be with Jesus *in 2018*, and his friend *Ron Matson (who did his eulogy)* read a sign that hung over Mr. Missler's desk that read, *"God doesn't give us another day for our own benefit, but for someone else's."* I'm not glorifying a man but rather, I am grateful for his obedience. Dr. Missler had a vision one evening that told him to: *"Stay the course."* Thank you all so much! *The world will miss you! Lastly, special thanks are due to those who gave their time to read or edit my manuscript. Your honesty, suggestions, and advice helped me refine my ideas as I was writing this book.*

> **"But none of these things move me, neither count I my life dear unto myself so that I might finish my course with joy, and the ministry, which I have received of the Lord Jesus, to testify the gospel of the grace of God."**

Acts 20:24

Chapter 1

INTRODUCTION

MAN, WROTE the Bible**! *I KNOW** I'm a good person**! HOW*** *can you know which version is RIGHT?* **NO one** *can* **EVER** *make me a sheep!* I **DON'T** *need* to go to church to be saved! *I DON'T need some organized religion that believes they are so high and mighty to tell me how to live my life!* **Preachers just want your MONEY!** *God is just a means of overcoming your* **fear of DEATH!** *What about all of those* **"ARCHAIC"** *words? I know there* **IS** *a God!* **OH, I've read the Bible! I'm Religious,** *but in my own way!*

I have said all of these things! All of these statements are totally expected responses towards today's modern Christians. The problem isn't the people who make these statements. The problem is our religious *"Christians"* in the body of Christ, that misrepresent our Father in Heaven. We may be the only Bible that non-believers ever read! These people may be in jails, bars, night clubs or even worse, they are stuck in non-word based (*Christian*) organizations that are saying, *"God Spoke to me,"* yet the words spoken don't line up with scripture. *God's "Word" and His "Spirit"* **cannot** *be separated! This is absolutely not God's*

1

plan! The religious groups and individuals within them are doing terrible damage to the body of Christ! This is just another example of why so many people reject the church. These same people eventually are led completely away from the church because of what *(false prophets)* may have led them to believe. *We as faithful believers may be the only thing that prevents people from stepping off the cliff, rather than being the one thing that leads them back from the edge!* We must express our love for truth by actions based upon our acceptance, right where they stand. People should look at Christians and be totally drawn to something special about them, even when we don't know what that something is! *We should look like Jesus!* We are made in His image. Love them! Show them our Savior!

> *"Let us not therefore judge one another any more: but judge this rather, that no man put a stumbling block or an occasion to fall in his brother's way."*

Romans 14:13

Let's begin our journey of shattering religion and its ugly relatives *(lies, legalism, myths, rumors, folklore and tradition.)* I'll explain why I chose the *1611 KJV* Bible as my reference. We'll see the hand of God and the love of *Jesus Christ* on every single page. We will discuss some things that you will either completely ignore and stop reading, or your eyes will be opened wide! We first have to build your faith in the Word of God, and why it is found in the King James Bible. I'm sure you'll agree, by the time we get through multiple presuppositions regarding religion, you'll understand why we need to decide which Bible is Truth. *Here we Go!*

Chapter 2

SHATTERING LIES, TRADITION AND RELIGION

There is a hidden message for those of you who read this book from the beginning to the end without skipping ahead. The Book of Revelation is much the same way and the only book that promises a *special blessing* to its readers!

> *"Blessed is he that readeth, and they that hear the words of this prophecy, and keep those things which are written therein: for the time is at hand."*-Revelation 1:31

My book is nothing like the Bible, although it will reveal the integrity of it in a way that you may have never noticed before. If you're not willing to see yourself transparently, (*as painful as it may be,*) then I recommend you toss this book in the nearest trash can immediately! My intention is to *lovingly* and humbly expose the truth of religion using *only* the Word of God! Don't take *anyone's* word for it. Examine the Word of God for yourself! Ask yourself if there is sin inside of you that is stinging by the *salt* of God's Word?

> *"Salt is good: but if the salt have lost his salt-*
> *ness, wherewith will ye season it? Have salt in*
> *yourselves, and have peace one with another."*
> -Mark 9:50

God is clearly comparing *salt (which is a preservative, that is meant to preserve the spirit*) to our own sin. This could easily be showing us that truth preserves the soul. Our conviction is burned by the salt of the truth! For those in pursuit of God's truth concerning the Word, I highly recommend ignoring the religious nonsense which has been vomited into the ears of the world. One definition of religion is *(a particular system of faith and worship.) Religion is the* reason why Jesus Christ ended up on the cross, to begin with! By the way, Jesus was a Jew, not a Christian. *BIG* shocker, right? *Not really,* considering the Bible refers to Christians as *(followers of Jesus)* according to G5547 of the Strong's Concordance. *Acts 11:26* states that disciples in Antioch were first called Christians because they followed Jesus so closely and were known to be *(like)* Jesus himself. Jesus was called, **"The Christ"** or (*Anointed One.*) The others were called *Christians*!

We are going to take a journey together that may surprise you. I'll provide you with Biblical doctrine that will have you thinking differently after you finish reading this book. Please go into prayer first with an open mind and listen carefully. I recommend that you follow along with a copy of the KJV Bible and search for yourself as we spend time together. Imagine you and me spending time reading this book so you *(the reader)* can get to know the author. *No, No, No*, I'm kidding !! *Get to know **Jesus!*** My point is how can we know someone intimately if we just glance at them once in a while and take them at face value? If I wrote my name in messy cursive and asked you what it said, you would say, *"I have no idea!"* If I printed my name, then you could easily read it. Jesus made this point in the book of Matthew 13:10-13 " V.*10*

> *"And the disciples came, and said unto him, Why*
> *speakest thou unto them in parables? V.11 He*

4

answered and said unto them, Because it is given unto you to know the mysteries of the kingdom of heaven, but to them it is not given. V.12 For whosoever hath, to him shall be given, and he shall have more abundance: but whosoever hath not, from him shall be taken away even that he hath. V.13 Therefore speak I to them in parables: because they seeing see not, and hearing they hear not, neither do they understand."-Matthew 13:10-13

He is quite simply saying, (In MY understanding,) that a deeper understanding of the scriptures will be given to those who hear it and receive it, rather than reject it!

Take your time and pace yourself, and meditate on the words and listen. I hope you're ready. That's the very first step to an amazing revelation before going any further! We are about to discuss the most important words ever given to humanity! *"The Word of God."*

THE GATEKEEPERS OF RELIGION

The Gatekeepers of our school systems and news media are the political, religious, and financial forces that control the flow of information. This information is then filtered into the minds and the souls of society. We are constantly bombarded with hype, slander, plagiarism, and propaganda. We are subtly controlled by a governing body that sits in a higher seat. Someone else you may have heard of, was called *subtle,* in the Bible.

> *"Now the serpent was more subtle than any beast of the field which the Lord God had made. And he said unto the woman, Yea, hath God said, Ye shall not eat of every tree of the garden?"*-Genesis 3:1

Back to my point about *"holding a higher seat!"*

5

God never wanted government because He was sending the one true king, but as we read in Samuel (*we saw it differently,*) so we elected our own king!

> *"And said unto him, Behold, thou art old, and thy sons walk not in thy ways: now make us a king to judge us like all the nations. But the thing displeased Samuel, when they said, Give us a king to judge us. And Samuel prayed unto the Lord. And the Lord said unto Samuel, Hearken unto the voice of the people in all that they say unto thee: for they have not rejected thee, but they have rejected me, that I should not reign over them."*-1 Samuel 8:5-7

These governing bodies, which are put in place by the general public (*that's you and me*), are established to rule over the world in all three of these areas. These are the Gatekeepers. The Gatekeepers throughout the Bible were called *(Porters.)* When Jesus asked Peter. *"Peter, who do you say I am?"* Peter said, *"You are The Christ!"* Peter wasn't listening to what the (*Gatekeepers)* were saying! The Gatekeepers or *religious* people were saying that Jesus was *(John the Baptist, and other prophets.)* The gatekeepers are the ones who have committed to sitting at the microphone and delivering lies. Even the leaders during the days of Jesus were arguing over religion!

> *"Then arose certain of the synagogue, which is called the synagogue of the Libertines, and Cyrenians, and Alexandrian, and of them of Cilicia and of Asia, disputing with Stephen."*-Acts 6:9

One day satan's time will run out and every child of God will talk again. The gatekeepers bully God's people into conformity. Their day was just like our day. They hated each other, just like politicians and nation leaders of today hate one another. *"Democrat"* or *"Republican,"* the *north* or the *south*, this all leads to one final outcome; division, hatred, and death. I want to leave you with one final thought. If you take a look at all major wars through-out history you would notice one thing that you may have noticed before. There has never been a true (*major*) holy war. It's my observation *(based upon the world we live in and the direction the world is heading)* that we will continue to have a war over *whose God is right!*

The book of Matthew, states what the "*Local News*" of the day was saying Jesus was a bad guy!

> *"When Jesus came into the coasts of Caesarea Philippi, he asked his disciples, saying, Whom do men say that I the Son of man am? And they said, "Some say that thou art John the Baptist: some, Elias; and others, Jeremias, or one of the prophets."* -Matthew 16:13-14

This is why so much widespread hatred for Jesus was circulated in the first place. Jesus asked Peter this question.

> *"He saith unto them, But whom say ye that I am?* -Matthew 16:15

Peter responded in Matthew "*And Simon Peter answered and said, Thou art the Christ, the Son of the Living God."* -Matthew 16:16

Jesus tells Peter that flesh and blood (*The Gatekeepers*) weren't saying that, but His Father (God) must have told him that, because the popular opinion was different!

> *"And Jesus answered and said unto him, Blessed art thou, Simon Barjona: for flesh and blood hath not revealed it unto thee, but my Father which is in heaven."* -Matthew 16:17

Peter was listening to GOD, not a popular religious opinion! Even the leaders during that day were arguing over religion!

> *"Then arose certain of the synagogue, which is called the synagogue of the Libertines, and Cyrenians, and Alexandrian, and of them of Cilicia and of Asia, disputing with Stephen."*-Acts 6:9

PHARISEE DECEPTION

So as we enter into the second chapter of this book, I realized that there are *two* types of readers. *Believers* and *spectators*. Let me explain starting with the religious leaders of that day. I suppose you expected me to say, *believers and nonbelievers.*

Nicodemus was a religious leader during the time of Jesus. He represented a group of Jewish sectors of the law that believed they were superior to everyone. They believed in the resurrection of Jesus Christ. They also believed in the traditions of their forefathers. Pharisee means to *"separate"* or *"separated ones."* Jesus is talking to the Pharisees.

> *"But woe unto you, scribes and Pharisees, hypocrites! For ye shut up the kingdom of heaven against men: for ye neither go into yourselves, neither suffer ye them that are entering to go in,"*
> -In Matthew 23:13

Jesus is warning here with*"Woe."* Jesus is saying that the Pharisees are causing men and women to reject Jesus. They are causing the Kingdom of God to be stained by religion, which turns the hearts of men against God! It is interesting to note as you read about the Pharisees, God allows Nicodemus's name to be mentioned several times in the New Testament. Nothing in the Bible is by accident. *"When we come across patterns or difficult passages we should rejoice!"(as Chuck Missler would say) "This is good."* Why would God allow so much air time, mentioning such a religious man? *(I believe)* The Bible is written in such a way that God typically uses what is called, *(The Law of First Mention.)* That is to say, He tends to reference very important things first, in priority, with a purpose. *Here is an example:*

> **"And he said, Take now thy son, thine only son Isaac, whom thou lovest, and get thee into the land of Moriah; and offer him there for a burnt offering upon one of the mountains which I will tell thee of."**-Genesis 22:2

There is a very important story here. God tells Abraham to sacrifice his own son, but as we know in the later verses, God will make Abraham put down the knife.

The Bible makes a spiritual parallel here through Abraham's obedience. God called Abraham *His friend.*

> **"And the scripture was fulfilled which saith, Abraham believed God, and it was imputed unto him for righteousness: and he was called the Friend of God"**- James 2:23

He was *the* friend, not *a* friend. I also find it interesting that God uses His law of first mention here. The word *"love"* is used for the very first time when He could have mentioned it anywhere in creation before Genesis *22.* God chose an allegory to express his love. God makes a comparison of Jesus being sacrificed. God is saying that there is no greater love than a man who lays down his life for a friend.

> **"Greater <u>love</u> hath no man than this, that a man lay down his life for his friends."**–John 15:13

So God wanted His friend Abraham to see the pain of losing a son, yet did not allow Abraham to actually lose his son. God wanted Abraham to see *(like a good friend would do)* what Jesus was about to go through at Calvary. He brought his son Abraham along to witness what He was about to allow Jesus to go through, in order to express his own love toward us. He uses love here first because it was the ultimate love, sacrifice. It's the first mention in the Bible.

Another thing in scripture I've noticed is that God would not have invested much air time with someone like (*Nicodemus*) unless God was intending to use him to express a spiritual truth! It is easy to read stories from the Bible, pass them down to our children in various churches, yet we ourselves haven't even looked at every word! Let us make this observation about Nicodemus and the Pharisees; it's possible God wanted us to look deeper into this story. *Stay with me, please!*

These *two* groups would show up to hear Jesus preach and wait to find fault in His message (*as many do today.*) They could have listened and gotten a powerful message that could have changed their lives, but instead, they showed up with a *"red* pen" hoping to find judgment in His Words. **"Don't we do this so often today?"** We use our two ears to receive a message that is life-changing, yet the first thing we tend to do is (*hear*) rather than (*listen*). So often we just hear and interject our judgment rather than listen and receive the message.

SADDUCEES

Sadducees were a different religious group of Jewish leaders, who denied the resurrection of the dead to include Jesus. They denied the existence of spirits and the obligation of oral traditions. They accepted the written law entirely, and alone. An easy way to remember Sadducees is they didn't believe Jesus resurrected, so they were, *"Sad You See."* The interesting thing about this group is the Bible never mentioned one single Sadducees ever being saved or redeemed. God has very little to say about the Sadducees at all. Nicodemus was mentioned several times, and he will play a huge role in understanding the purpose of God's Word.

We do know the Pharisees and Sadducees couldn't stand one another, but they equally agreed they needed to get rid of Jesus as well as those who believed in Him. They both feared the people might begin to follow Jesus and disregard their religious rules and beliefs (*Causing them to lose total control.*) This reminds me of Democrats and Republicans. They fight each other for leadership but join forces to get rid of Jesus in the public sector! Hmmm.

RELIGION LEADS TO RACISM AND HOLY WAR

Our country, on so many worldwide platforms, is plagued by inequality, race and gender discrimination. Most of these differences boil down to people controlling our social media platforms, religious organizations, and our economic heavy hitters. We have turned man into God and have become *the created* worshipping *(the created)* instead of *(the created)* worshipping the *Creator! These people always say,* "*oh mother earth.*" God made the earth and we are *not* to worship any other man. God *made* man! *We* should worship only the maker! *This is very clear!*

> "*Thou shalt have no other gods before me. Thou shalt not make unto thee any graven image, or any likeness of any thing that is in heaven above, or that is in the earth beneath, or that is in the water under the earth. Thou shalt not bow down thyself to them, nor serve them: for I the Lord thy God am a jealous God, visiting the iniquity of the fathers upon the children unto the third and fourth generation of them that hate me;*"-
> Exodus 20:3-5

We have become exactly what Adam and Eve became when they listened to the serpent in Genesis.

> "*For God doth know that in the day ye eat thereof, then your eyes shall be opened, and ye shall be as gods, knowing good and evil.*"- Genesis 3:5

It was here that satan would tell Eve that she could be a god. In the book of *Matthew 24:7,* Jesus makes a very *well known statement.*

> **"For nation shall rise against nation, and kingdom against kingdom: and there shall be famines, and pestilences, and earthquakes, in divers places."**-Matthew 24:7

Jesus is saying that the world is slowly falling apart and there will be *hunger-incurable diseases and earthquakes from underwater & nations against nations.* This word, *"nation"* is translated from the Greek word *"Ethnos"* which means *"Ethnicity."* This would mean Jesus is saying that *ethnicity would be against ethnicity!* Jesus also mentions *"kingdom against kingdom,"* the word kingdom is not used in the literal term that we would so often assume. This word *kingdom* was translated from its original form, from the word *"basileia,"* which means *royal or power.* The enemy will use the people who control the flow of information to persuade the minds of the people and cause mass division, which spreads anger and confusion. Why not pick another nationality, race, political party member, or someone who doesn't sound like you or talk like you? The enemy knows that he can't kill us himself, so he causes us to kill one another! All he has to do is lead both opposing parties in two different directions and make one think the other caused it. Here's the sad part. If both parties actually sat down, discussed their differences, and kept the enemy's deception out of it, they'd probably hear each other's side of the story. Things would be so beautiful if we would just ignore the voice of the tempter.

Chapter 3

THE BIBLE IS THE FINAL AUTHORITY

WHY BELIEVE THE BIBLE and why THE KING JAMES?

New Testament books were written shortly after the time of Christ. Copies had to be made which on average would take (*10-12*) months by hand in mainly scroll form. The Scribes had very effective methods of preserving the text in its entirety. All of these copies were spread throughout the world. This was a time of great persecution. Christians were definitely hated in this time period. Copies would have been preserved and eventually, over the years they would have deteriorated. A well-kept manuscript would last roughly *200-400* years when used actively every day. By the time each scroll or book had worn out, new ones had already been replenished. This process wouldn't have mattered because multiple copies would have already been remade using the same preservation process as the last. As a matter of fact, the Scribes would take special care when transliterating each letter. It was customary that they would even count how many "*a's,*" from the *left*, or from the *right*, to get it perfectly written. Here's an example. If there were seven letters in one direction rather than eight, they would start over from scratch. Damaged copies would have to be burned, or even buried. They were very strict! These were (*exact*) copies and then copies of copies, and so on. This method was exactly the same for several generations resulting in thousands of copies being put into circulation still today. In the 1500s they decided to print the Bible in English. *Erasmus, Luther, Tyndale,* and the *Geneva* Bibles, are all examples of this. These versions were translated into English. Roughly *5909* copies from all over the world were found. These groups of manuscripts became known in Latin as the *(Texus Receptus)* or (*The Received Text.)* Besides the spelling of cities or people's names such as *Paul, Saul, Peter or Pedro, etc.* (*roughly 4 to 5 percent.)* They could find no differences whatsoever! The English translations became known as the *(Majority Text,)* commonly known today as the *King James Bible*, completed and printed in *1611*.

In the meantime there was a cult group in Alexandria, Egypt called the Alexandrians who had a major library in a large city. They had a lot of strange beliefs and decided to take scrolls and make little changes here and there to better suit their belief system. Many verses were left out. The primary guy in charge of this Alexandrian Bible was named *(Origin 240 A.D)*. In *350 A.D.)* Two copies of the Alexandrian Bibles made are called the *Codex Sinaiticus* because they were found in the Sinai Desert in a Vatican monastery. In *380 A.D*, these copies were translated into Latin and were called the *(Latin Vulgate 1582.)* The Catholic Church ordered the translation of the Latin Vulgate, into English. This is where the Catholic Douay Rheims Bible came into print. This became a very good translation of the **wrong** manuscripts that came from the Alexandrian Manuscripts! The Catholic (*Douay Rheims Version)* is used today and includes *(7)* extra books that are not found in the King James Version totaling *(73)* books rather than *(66)* here is a list of them *(Tobit, Judith, Baruch, Wisdom, Sirach, 1 and 2 Maccabees, and parts of Esther and Daniel)*.

Two men named Westcott and Hort came along in approximately *1875* and took these Alexandrian manuscripts and assumed since they were older, they must be better. They were *older but worse copies* because they were inaccurate and never used enough to be worn out! They were bad copies! They made this modern Greek addition in *1875* into English. These versions would include (*the Revised Version) in 1881, The American Standard Version in 1901, The Revised Standard in 1946, The New World Translation or Jehovah's Witness Version in 1950, the New American Standard in 1960, Good News Bible, the Amplified Bible, and eventually the NIV)* All of these are wonderful translations of the **wrong** manuscripts! *1600 years later, they are still around today!*

Before moving on, I want to mention something that has always been misunderstood. Remember that *A.D.* and *B.C.* thing you were always taught in school? Well, it's not "*before Christ*" and"*After Death.*" This actually means before Christ and *(Anno Domini)* or, *In the year of the Lord. Go dig for yourself!*

After several years and thousands of hours of research, it's been discovered that our Greek manuscripts were documented by hundreds of eyewitnesses, during the lifetime of *other eyewitnesses, and testified of their findings within months of the actual resurrection taking place!* Even if you still choose to ignore the facts because they seem so far fetched, then you would be hard-pressed to trust any history book you've ever read! Wouldn't this mean that every other man-made book must be a lie and couldn't be trusted? The story of Jesus and what He did for us takes more faith **not** to believe! Tell me, if you looked at a cell phone *200* years ago and saw a human talking on it, you would think you were seeing a demon? Of course, you would, because at that point your understanding is primitive. Just because our little brains aren't developed into knowing the mysteries of God doesn't mean He isn't real. I usually ask non-believers this question.

What is love for your child? And they respond, "*huh?*"

What is love? Show it to me? Let me touch it?

And they would say, "I can't!" I would say, "Wait, if you can't, then you must not feel anything toward your child?"

If you can't see the love or touch the love, and it (has no weight or mass) then it must not exist? *wrong*! God is love and He is not bound by any of these attributes. He lives outside of time and is eternal. Just because He doesn't contain physical properties that we don't understand, doesn't mean He isn't real. He sent His only son in the flesh so He could communicate His love to us!

"For God so loved the world, that he gave his only begotten Son, that whosoever believeth in him should not perish, but have everlasting life."- John 3:16

All of the information I have provided is physical, provable, and documented on planet earth today. You don't have to believe in flying saucers, religious practices, or even an angelic man, who was called the Son of God if you don't wish to. If you believe textbooks and allow your children to learn the opinions of history, then why on earth would you ignore the same documents and proven written facts? I am simply providing you what my research has shown me up until now.

I believe that the Bible is the unchanged, infallible, unadulterated perfect Word of our Living God. There is an old classroom game called *(Chinese Whispers,)* or *(Telephone,)* in *Western English,* where a line of children would whisper a statement into the ear of the other. By the time the word made it to the last person's ear, the entire story would change. This exercise involves just a few children with simple messages. By the time the message made it to the end of the line, the entire story, and its context, would change. Imagine how quickly their stories changed, just within a few minutes, and realize how amazing, in comparison, the King James Bible is because it has not changed! All of the information I have provided is physical, provable, and documented on planet earth today. You don't have to believe in flying saucers, religious practices, or even an angelic man, who was called the Son of God if you don't wish to. If you believe textbooks and allow your children to learn the opinions of history, then why on earth would you ignore the same documents and proven written facts? I am simply providing you what my research has shown me up until now.

The point I'm making about the KJV Bible is that it was passed down over thousands of years, flawlessly. These collections were discovered in over *3* continents. *(Asia, Africa and Europe)* in at least *3* different languages, *(Hebrew, Greek, and a bit of Aramaic.)* Most of the writers, if not all of them, never met. There were *(prophets, priests, kings, business men, shepherds, lawyers, physicians, tax collectors, preachers, fishermen, generals, doctors, historians and soldiers, etc.) None of these different people had any idea that what they were writing would end up in our modern Bible copies today*! There are *sixty six* volumes of writings, covering hundreds and hundreds of subjects, and they all perfectly matched except certain names that don't even exist today!

I would like to bring something to your attention. There were over *301* eyewitnesses in the Bible who were actual witnesses while Jesus was still alive! (*During the time 1st Corinthians was written.*) Paul's claims were falsifiable claims and they could have been easily tested but were still ***not*** falsified! This is very important to note. They have *never* been falsified! Of course we have people like Constantine and others who make claims. So often men tried to find religious ways to explain the perfect preservation of His book and have over time tried to explain every way to discredit its authority. If (*KJV*) only advocated and decided to believe that the English translation was the Word of God, then eventually people would find fault in that. *Here's the thing*, it wouldn't matter which version was considered the true one. I think the problem is that man cannot sign on to the fact that there is one perfect Bible. It's funny to me that the same people who believe that a man died, came back to life, and floated through the air (*ascended into heaven*) but don't believe the same God wrote His Word perfectly and preserved it! The truth is, the reason so many people reject the Bible in *(my opinion,)* is that if we believed the writings in it, then the Bible would become a personal glaring mirror that would force us to change how we live our lives! *Dr. Voddie Baucham* said it best, *"We have a reliable collection of historical documents written down by eyewitnesses, during the lifetime of other eyewitnesses who report supernatural events that took place in fulfillment of specific prophecies and claim that their writings are divine rather than human in their origin."*

THE LIE-TWISTING THE WORD

From the foundation of the time, the Bible has been the most produced and purchased book on earth. On average based on what I have found, over *100 million* Bibles are printed every year; *25* percent of which are purchased right here in the U.S. There are over *80,000* different versions of the Bible which generate sales annually! It is estimated by the *Guinness Book of World Records* that at least *five billion* Bibles have been printed to date. Good business right! Well I suppose that depends on whether or not you want to spread the accurate Word of God or you want to generate the most income! It's no secret that the Bible has taken on its own ecosystem and has been mis-used for proprietary motives. This is where I will draw the first analysis of *religion*. Here we go. According to my research, the copyright law when publishing books, requires that *30 %* of something written must be changed to republish a new version of it. This raises a question in my mind. God says in the book of Revelation 22:19 KJV version:

> *"And if any man shall take away from the words of the book of this prophecy, God shall take away his part out of the book of life, and out of the holy city, and from the things which are written in this book."*-Revelation 22:19

We have to ask ourselves the question, *(if)* we are required to change at least *30* percent of the words in the Bible to get them published, then we have to make quite a few changes to get these things published to make money. Here's the second problem. How do we get more sales? *(Hmmm)* We first have to change *30* percent of the original scripture and have to include things that would sell more Bibles...maybe we could leave out things that may offend a prospective buyer?

Now that I have your full attention I would like to mention something that blew my mind when I discovered it! It turns out that those changes in other Bibles went far beyond a few small changes. If you look at many modern Bibles today you will notice something very interesting. For example, I was stunned to discover that there were entire *verses that are* just completely **gone**! *Literally, 16 were **left out**!* Here is a list

> *"Howbeit this kind goeth not out but by prayer and fasting."*-Matthew 17:21

> *"For the Son of man is come to save that which was lost."*- Matthew 18:11

> *"Woe unto you, scribes and Pharisees, hypocrites! for ye devour widows' houses, and for a pretence make long prayer: therefore ye shall receive the greater damnation."*-Matthew 23:14

> *"If any man have ears to hear, let him hear."*-Mark 7:16

> *"Where their worm dieth not, and the fire is not quenched."*-Mark 9:44

> *"Where their worm dieth not, and the fire is not quenched."*-Mark 9:46

> *"But if ye do not forgive, neither will your Father which is in heaven forgive your trespasses."*-Mark 11:26

"And the scripture was fulfilled, which saith, And he was numbered with the transgressors."-Mark 15:28

"Two men shall be in the field; the one shall be taken, and the other left."-Luke 17:36

"For an angel went down at a certain season into the pool, and troubled the water: whosoever then first after the troubling of the water stepped in was made whole of whatsoever disease he had."-John 5:4

"And Philip said, If thou believest with all thine heart, thou mayest. And he answered and said, I believe that Jesus Christ is the Son of God."- Acts 8:37

"Notwithstanding it pleased Silas to abide there still."-Acts 15:34

"But the chief captain Lysias came upon us, and with great violence took him away out of our hands,"-Acts 24:7

"And when he had said these words, the Jews departed, and had great reasoning among themselves."-Acts 28:29

"The grace of our Lord Jesus Christ be with you all. Amen."-Romans 16:24

If God wanted us to add or take away words then why did He write this in Revelation!

"For I testify unto every man that heareth the words of the prophecy of this book, If any man

shall add unto these things, God shall add unto him the plagues that are written in this book:"-Revelation 22:18

MEN TRANSLATED IT! ANOTHER CLAIM THAT MAKES NO SENSE!

"Well, it's been translated so many times!" I've heard this over and over again and *it's absolutely ridiculous!"* Let me explain why. Let's say that my notepad *represented* the original Hebrew scrolls. You were a translator who came to get my notes, and translated them into your language, and handed them to every person in your town. The next thing you would do is hand my notes to a mayor in a different town who handed them to all of his citizens in the same fashion. After several years you would have given several different mayors my notes. After many years, thousands of mayors all over the world would possess my original notes. All of their notes would still originate from my hands and should be identical. Religion has taught us that I handed one note to you, and you reworded them and handed them to another and they reworded them and handed them to another, and so on. As time went on, each note would be altered, rewritten and would eventually end up corrupt. Eventually my notes would be changed because the people stopped coming back to me for the original copies. The truth is, I handed you the original. All original copies would still come from my hands each time. My copy was still the authority and all of the Mayors came back to me. *"The King James Bible,"* *was* transliterated in the very same way! The other thing I want to make clear is that we can (still today) go to the original Hebrew text, which was perfectly re-documented with exact precision. The King James writers were completely monitored and confirmed their writings for the purity of their exact original text. In most cases the reader doesn't learn Hebrew and Greek to confirm this truth. They just adopt and trust that the book they were told about, is true. This is the problem. God himself told us to search the scripture!

"It is the glory of God to conceal a thing: but the honour of kings is to search out a matter."-Proverbs 25:2

"Search the scriptures; for in them ye think ye have eternal life: and they are they which testify of Me."-John 5:39

It's one thing to have almost *6000* copies. In case you don't believe me I will guide you to Luke's Gospel where he wrote *not* from the perspective of meeting Jesus, but women actually gave accounts to him. During that time, women were not even allowed to speak. I would think that if this were all made up, we wouldn't see accounts of women's testimonies for the simple fact that no one during that time would have believed them! Like most other religions, this is not one man claiming these things. This is a man who admits not knowing Jesus personally. He is saying there is a collection of documents.

I have an interesting thought for you. Other historical books have been written throughout time that are widely taught and trusted as the truth in our school systems, and we accept them. We do have actual historical Biblical documents today that date back to roughly *100-120 AD*, within a decade of the completion of the New Testament. On the other hand there are less than a dozen of Aristotle's poetics and we can only go back to within *1000* years of the writings. Julius Caesar (*Gallic Wars*) again had only less than a dozen copies still available today. We can go back within a thousand years; between the last writings and the first manuscripts; and physically put our hands on them. When you look at Homer's Iliad, there are many more still available (*only a couple hundred.*) The other problem is that they are only dated back *2100* years after they were written. This seems absolutely insane to me, considering there are so few of these stories available and yet there are over *5000* portions of Greek manuscripts of the Bible that are traced back to Paul's New Testament writings, which perfectly match *and are* researched, confirmed and tested as well as documented from all the authors prior to that. Even after all of this careful work, people still say, *"Well, we don't have enough proof."* I'll say this more than once to you who believe in some elaborate scheme; *come on!* I want to go one step further.

POPULAR RELIGIOUS BELIEFS TO REJECT THE GOSPEL

> *"All scripture is given by inspiration of God, and is profitable for doctrine, for reproof, for correction, for instruction in righteousness:"*-2 Timothy 3:16

God was able to preserve His Holy Word! His Word was prophesied long before Jesus was born, and was written by witnesses in the lifetime of other eyewitnesses and was self-validated.

> *"If I bear witness of myself, my witness is not true."*- John 5:31

> *"Search the scriptures; for in them ye think ye have* **eternal life: and they are they which testify of me.**"-John 5:39

Then I will openly and easily believe what has been confirmed throughout history. I have no problem believing that God inspired every word of the Bible and moved the hands of man in doing so.

I'VE NEVER HEARD OF JESUS, AM I GOING TO HELL?

> *"Because that which may be known of God is manifest in them; for God hath shewed it unto them."*-Romans 1:19

God is revealed through His Creation! This is ridiculous! Religion says that if they didn't know Jesus, then either the Bible is lying or Jesus wasn't really the Messiah. Unfortunately, non-believers will find any reason to tear down the Word of God. It's more important to know the truth, and come into the knowledge of God! *Don't listen to man!*

> *"The Heavens declare the glory of God; and firmament sheweth his handywork.""Day unto day uttereth speech, and night sheweth knowledge.*
>
> *There is no speech nor language, where their voice is not heard.*
>
> *Their line is gone out through all the earth, and their words to the end of the world.*
>
> *In them hath he set a tabernacle for the sun, Which is as a bridegroom coming out of his chamber, and rejoiceth as a strong man to run a race. His going forth is from the end of heaven, and his circuit unto the ends of it: and there is nothing hid from the heat thereof.*
>
> *The law of the Lord is perfect, converting the soul: the testimony of the Lord is sure, making wise the simple. The statutes of the Lord are right, rejoicing the heart: the commandment of the Lord is pure, enlightening the eyes."*-Psalm 19:1-8

If you understand how the Bible is written and what God is saying, then you will understand the scripture when you read

> *"For God so loved the world, that he gave his only begotten Son, that whosoever believeth in him should not perish, but have everlasting life."*- John 3:16

This verse is displaying God's love for us, using a parallel between (*Abraham and Isaac*) vs (*God and Jesus.*) It is clearly showing us God's perfect love towards us!

> **"And Abraham stretched forth his hand, and took the knife to slay his son."**-Genesis 22:10

> *"And the angel of the Lord called unto him out of heaven, and said, Abraham, Abraham: and he said, Here am I."*- Genesis 22:11

It's very likely that Abraham was redeemed, even though Jesus hadn't been born yet. God has obviously made His presence known with signs and seasons throughout creation! You can decide for yourself.

PEOPLE MUST HAVE ALTERED THE SCRIPTURES SECRETLY?

Constantine was the first Roman Emperor to convert to Christianity. He played an influential role in the proclamation of the Edict of Milan in *313*, which declared tolerance for Christianity in the Roman Empire. If monks of this time period were to pull off this elaborate scheme of altering the scriptures, they needed to find *around six thousand* Greek manuscripts and portions of manuscripts, and change all of them exactly the same way, without being caught. They couldn't have told anyone what they were up to, or what they did. The next couple of centuries later, the manuscripts would be translated in the (*Siriac, Coptic and Latin*) languages. The next problem is they would have had to lie about it because they couldn't have matched the other language from the previous Greek, and Hebrew languages, etc. This meant they would have changed the originals without getting caught doing so. All of this would have happened throughout all of the languages. Another thing to consider is the early church fathers wrote extensive commentaries and writings of what they saw. At this point, this huge conspiracy would include all this ink work, (*even the*

25

old commentaries) as well as the *(stolen and changed ones)* and they would have to put all of them back in the exact same places. This elaborate scheme would have had to take place within *1500* plus years, with absolutely *No mistakes* in the preservation process! This is obviously *not* possible! I Don't want you to take my word for the King James Bible because I said so, but I definitely don't want you to believe that the King James Bible isn't the final authority because someone else said so! There have been well over *25,000* excavational dig sites related to this subject and not even one single dig has **_ever_** contradicted the Bible! As a matter of fact, they usually **confirm** the Bible even more!

RELIGION SAYS *"WE TRUST SCIENCE"*

It is ridiculous to conceive that large scale fraud was possible. Yes, these manuscripts were written by men, but inspired by God himself. Some people say, *(I need scientific proof!)* This always makes me wonder if they are either uneducated on science, foolish, or maybe realize that if it's true, it would force them to change their ways! Science believes that if something is *1.) Observable 2.) Measurable 3.) Repeatable, then it's scientific!*

The Bible is none of this, *because it is a history book*! We would use *(evidentiary methods)* much like court proceedings would use. Are the documents reliable? Is there evidence collectively agreed upon? Is it reputable or has provable evidence on both sides by witnesses collectively? Is it falsifiable? If you ask these questions, *(just like in a courtroom,)* and the answer is yes, then you will have no choice but to conclude that using the same methods, commonly used in all of our *(Judicial Systems)* are reliable and the Bible *can* be trusted! It can be trusted because it's a reliable collection of historical documents, written down by eyewitnesses, during the lifetime of other eyewitnesses, and reported supernatural events that took place in fulfilment of specific prophecies and claimed that their writings are divine, rather than human in origin!

If you choose not to believe any of this, then every single history book and courtroom decision ever made, must be thrown out and all criminals must be released, because we can no longer use provable resources!

> ***"All scripture is given by inspiration of God, and is profitable for doctrine, for reproof, for correction, for instruction in righteousness."***-2 Timothy 3:16

If you still are not convinced, then let me take you to *2 Peter 1:16.*

> ***"For we have not followed cunningly devised fables, when we made known unto you the power and coming of our Lord Jesus Christ, but were eyewitnesses of his majesty."***-2 Peter 1:16

> *V.17* ***"For he received from God the Father honour and glory, when there came such a voice to him from the excellent glory, This is my beloved Son, in whom I am well pleased."***

> *V.18* ***"And this voice which came from heaven we heard, when we were with him in the holy mount."***

> V.19 ***"We have also a more sure word of prophecy; whereunto ye do well that ye take heed, as unto a light that shineth in a dark place, until the day dawn, and the day star arise in your hearts:"***

> V.20 ***"Knowing this first, that no prophecy of the scripture is of any private interpretation."***

> V.21 ***"For the prophecy came not in old time by the will of man: but holy men of God spake as they were moved by the Holy Ghost."***

Luke is writing down *(actual)* statements in vs16 of *(Eye Witnesses,) V.17*, *(a voice)* being well pleased and in *V.18,* the voice out of the mount. *These were eyewitnesses!* I will further give you evidence of this proof that eye witnesses testified of. Check this out in *Luke 1:1.*

> *"Forasmuch as many have taken in hand to set forth in order a declaration of those things which are most surely believed among us, Even as they delivered them unto us, which from the beginning were eyewitnesses, and ministers of the word; It seemed good to me also, having had perfect understanding of all things from the very first, to write unto thee in order, most excellent Theophilus, That thou mightest know the certainty of those things, wherein thou hast been instructed."*-Luke 1:1-4

Luke *(known as a very prolific writer)* was very specific in his writings when reporting all that he had heard from Peter, Mary, etc. Luke was a master historian and obviously his gospel is not from the perspective of Jesus himself. Luke wrote extensively and accurately about what Paul and others told him about Jesus. He went to great lengths to write *(accurately)* what had happened!

Lets go to more scriptures written by Luke and Paul to send this point home!! *1 John 1:1-3.*

> *"That which was from the beginning, which we have heard, which we have seen with our eyes, which we have looked upon, and our hands have handled, of the Word of life;"*-1 John 1:1

> *"For the life was manifested, and we have seen it, and bear witness, and shew unto you that eternal life, which was with the Father, and was manifested unto us;"*-1 John 1:2

"That which we have seen and heard declare we unto you, that ye also may have fellowship with us: and truly our fellowship is with the Father, and with his Son Jesus Christ."-1 John 1:3

PAUL'S TRUE GOSPEL OF JESUS

"Moreover, brethren, I declare unto you the gospel which I preached unto you, which also ye have received, and wherein ye stand; By which also ye are saved, if ye keep in memory what I preached unto you, unless ye have believed in vain. For I delivered unto you first of all that which I also received, how that Christ died for our sins according to the scriptures; And that he was buried, and that he rose again the third day according to the scriptures: And that he was seen of Cephas, then of the twelve: After that, he was seen of above five hundred brethren at once; of whom the greater part remain unto this present, but some are fallen asleep. After that, he was seen of James; then of all the apostles. And last of all he was seen of me also, as of one born out of due time. For I am the least of the apostles, that am not meet to be called an apostle, because I perse-cuted the church of God." -1 Corinthians 15:1-9

This is where Paul drops the mic!!

Even the Apostle John *(who wrote the Gospel of John)* is saying he *saw and heard Jesus with his own eyes* from the beginning, and passed down his testimony. If you choose to still reject the truth, then nothing else will convince you!

4 GOSPELS

John's gospel was focused on the *seven* signs, and evangelism. He has passion! Mark's gospel was the shortest, only focusing on facts. He liked to use words like *"Straight way"* and *"in a hurry."* Matthew's gospel focused mainly on the lineage of how Jesus got here, which is why it was recorded back in the book of *Matthew 5. (Adam begot Seth and Seth begat Enoch and so forth.)* This chart will better outline for you how each of the tribe and Cherubims (*ex. lion, man, ox, and eagle*) and color.

Book # -Gospel	Symbol	Color	Tribe	Direction
40-Matthew-Jew	Lion	Purple	Judah	East
41-Mark-	OX	Red	Manassa	West
42-Luke-Gentile	Man	White	Ruebin	South
43-John-Jew	Eagle	Blue	Dan	North

	Writers Trade	Writer Audience	Writer calls Jesus	view point of Jesus
40-Matthew-Jew	Tax Collector	Young beliver	King of the Jews	What He said
41-Mark-	Evangelist	The unbeliever	Son of Man	What He did
42-Luke-Gentile	Physician	The unbeliever	Savior of the world	What He said
43-John-Jew	Fisherman	Mature believer	Son of God	Who He was

	Traces jesus back by	Gospel name means	Says Jesus is a	How writer died
40-Matthew-Jew	Birth Geneology Ch 5	Gift of the Lord	A King	Steaked/bheaded
41-Mark-	His baptism	John	A Servant	Drug by rope
42-Luke-Gentile	Beginning at Adam	Lover of God	A Man	Martyred/hanged
43-John-Jew	The beginning/Gen 1	God is gracious	God	natural causes

	Writers birth date	Writers death date	Writers Min location	Writers death locate
40-Matthew-Jew	1 AD	74 AD	Jerusalem	Ethipopia
41-Mark-	U/k	68 AD April 25	Galilee & Judea	Alexandria, Egypt
42-Luke-Gentile	1 AD	84 AD	Padula, Italy	Thiva, Greece
43-John-Jew	6AD	100 AD	Ephesus	Ephesus

	Writers birth locat.	Writers view from	Gospel origin date	Writers age at Death
40-Matthew-Jew	Galilee	Mary & women	80-90 AD	74
41-Mark-	Cyrene, Libya	Freinds	70 AD	62-63
42-Luke-Gentile	Antioc, Syria	Paul/ others	80-110 AD	84
43-John-Jew	Bethaida, Galilee	He was called friend	85-110 AD	93-94

This chart shows the four Gospels and their perspectives; biblical colors, tribes, directions. They will help paint a larger picture of Jesus

RELIGION IN ROME

I would ask that you would read this section of my book with a loving spirit and pursuit of truth. I need to make something clear. My intention is to raise your awareness of the gospel and beg you to look for yourself before adopting a belief system. You may be loyal to a church or group of churches, or traditions that have been passed down to you from your family. There is a common belief that a man has become the authority of worship in some of our well known religious establishments. Now I'm going to take you to the scripture that the majority of the Catholic Church is founded upon. Please know that it is not my motive to attack any particular denomination, but rather show you how often we can make the Gospel about edifying ourselves, rather than Jesus. Jesus asks Peter and the disciples a question just before going off to be crucified. He is gathered with his disciples and asks...

> *"When Jesus came into the coasts of Caesarea Philippi, he asked his disciples, saying, '' Whom do men say that I the Son of man am?"*-Matthew 16:13

Peter speaks up and says this...

> *"And Simon Peter answered and said, Thou art the Christ, the Son of the living God."*- Matthew 16:16

The people at this time were *all* persecuting and wanting to kill Jesus. The fact that Peter had a *revelation* of who He really Jesus really was, made Jesus very happy! Following this statement Jesus makes a response in the next verse. He says that *"People aren't saying this, so you must have a revelation from somewhere else and it must be from God!* Just listen and I'll get to my point here in *V.17.*

> *"And Jesus answered and said unto him, Blessed art thou, Simon Barjona: for flesh and blood hath*

> *not revealed it unto thee, but my Father which is in heaven."*- Matthew 16:17

No one had ever said that before! This was a new revelation, and it came to Peter. Jesus was happy that Peter (*even being the only one*) had faith. (*We all have this ability*) Don't get me wrong, Peter was an amazing man, but he had foot in mouth disease, more often than not. This time, Peter finally got it right! Read what comes next. (*Side note:*) Peter was called Simon until he came into covenant.

> *"And I say also unto thee, That thou art Peter, and upon this rock I will build my church; and the gates of hell shall not prevail against it."*-Matthew 16:18

So let me explain what just happened in this part of the Bible. Now you see Jesus calling *Simon* by the name *Peter.* This is interesting in Hebrew because God would assign a new name to anyone in covenant with Him. God would interject a mark, signifying (*Himself*) into the original Hebrew manuscripts, such as Saul becoming Paul and Abram becoming Abraham. I'll explain more as we keep reading. Getting back to my point, Jesus makes the statement, *"Thou art Peter, and upon this rock."*

The name "*Peter"* comes from the Greek word "*Petros,"* or (*stone or rock.*) The word *Petros is* rooted in the word *petroleum* or *what comes out of a rock.* It is more known as a pebble or part of a larger cornerstone. This may give some deeper understanding of why Jesus is saying you are a *part* of my rock.

> *"And did all drink the same spiritual drink: for they drank of that spiritual Rock that followed them: and that Rock was Christ."*-1 Corinthians 10:4

And Jesus goes on to say, *"I will build my church on (IT), or the knowledge of who I am."* : This is clearly referring to something else, right? *So what will Jesus build His church on?* Jesus was clearly saying that on that revelation of who you just said I am, that I will build my church! Or I will use you as one of the first men who sees Me, for who I really am, and I will appoint you to help me start my church! I'll put it another way. Jesus is honoring Peter, and adding His new name to the Book of Life. He is obviously not saying that Peter is to be worshipped. He is simply using a faithful man to advance His ministry before going off to die on the cross at Calvary. This is the same way He would use us to advance His kingdom today. *Peter was just one of the first and is just a man like us!* At this point Jesus will go on to say that the gates of hell shall not prevail against Him.

> **"And I will give unto thee the keys of the kingdom of heaven: and whatsoever thou shalt bind on earth shall be bound in heaven: and whatsoever thou shalt loose on earth shall be loosed in heaven."**-Matthew 16:19

This is very likely pointing to the story where Jacob, which means (*Israel*), the son of Isaac, had a dream of angels ascending and descending on a ladder as he slept on a rock in the desert and would later build a pillar representing the entryway into the Holy Land. I love mentioning this because it could very well be the "Gates of Heaven." You decide! I could spend all day on this. It's interesting to note that if Peter were in some"*Holy*"category, then he sure messed up quite a bit, like the rest of us. Peter denied Jesus, cut off a man's ear and tried to keep him from going to the cross. I think the point here is we get in the (*religious*) way too much!

> **"But he turned, and said unto Peter, Get thee behind me, Satan: thou art an offence unto me: for thou savourest not the things that be of God, but those that be of men."** -Matthew 16:23

Wait! Is Peter just a man who sins exactly like we do? Isn't it just like us today? We always try to change God's plan, because we think we have a better idea. I have one more thought before we go. *No one changes God's plans!* Just watch this verse.

> *"Then Simon Peter having a sword drew it, and smote the high priest's servant, and cut off his right ear. The servant's name was Malchus. Then said Jesus unto Peter, Put up thy sword into the sheath: the cup which my Father hath given me, shall I not drink it?"*-John 18:10-11

Once again we have a classic case of *loving Peter* trying to use *man made* efforts to help Jesus when He doesn't want our Works. He wants our faith! This will amaze you! Jesus never *ONE* time literally *(covers up)* a sin, up until this point. At this point in scripture, Jesus is being taken captive to be crucified, and Peter still tries to intervene. Jesus at this point has already been attacked by satan, using his friend Peter, when Jesus said, *"satan, get behind me,"* earlier. After Peter cuts off the ear of the soldier, Jesus restores it. Most people would see this as a kind deed to show the Roman soldiers that He loves them, but there is a more important message here *(I believe.)* It would seem that if Jesus would have covered Peter's mistake, then Peter would have been judged and ended up on the cross right alongside Jesus. This would have directly affected the starting of the church that he was appointed to be a part of. What you see here is Jesus doing what He must do, to advance the kingdom and to make his way to the cross for you and me. The point is, **no one** *changes God's plan! The Death of Jesus Christ was **not** a tragedy*, it was a success! The only tragedy is the fact that we forced Him into the situation to prove His love for us!

Again Peter makes a huge mistake while being asked if he knew who Jesus was as he was being crucified.

> *"Then saith the damsel that kept the door unto Peter, Art not thou also one of this man's disciples? He saith, I am not."*-John 18:17

"And Simon Peter stood and warmed himself. They said therefore unto him, Art not thou also one of his disciples? He denied it, and said, I am not."-John 18:25

"Peter then denied again: and immediately the cock crew.-John 18:27

SHOULD WE CALL ANYONE FATHER?

"And call no man your father upon the earth: for one is your Father, which is in heaven." You decide!-Matthew 23

Jesus said His final words in the book of John, in the *19*th chapter:

"When Jesus therefore had received the vinegar, He said, It is finished: and He bowed His head, and gave up the ghost."- John 19:30

This reminds me of, *"I am the First Tav!"*

Jesus was a Jewish boy and it was customary that any Jewish boy would celebrate their coming of age at 13 depending on whether they were a boy or a girl. This was a time that a boy was considered to be a man and he should go be with his father, yet even at such a young age, he understood where his true father was!

"And call no man your father upon the earth: for one is your Father, which is in heaven."- Matthew 23:9

Speaking of religion, are we supposed to call anyone Father? Jesus calls God Father!!

This ceremony was called *"Bar mitzvah"* bar meaning *Son or Son of,* and Mitzvah- meaning *commandments (or the law,)* easier

35

put (the *Son of the law.*) Every Jewish boy at thirteen, in Judaism, would have to learn the *Torah* or the first five books of the Bible and were required to read it aloud. Jesus is on assignment and He was here for a purpose. He was heaven sent and earth rejected! Jesus was sent in the form of a man. The word "form" means "*Morphe,* and is *the innermost part, that never changes! We can change our fashion but we can never change our form!*

Chapter 4

IT'S ALL ABOUT THE MORE, MARKS AND $

DO WE HAVE A PROSPERITY GOSPEL?

*P*rosperity gospel? This says your flesh gets to live!! This alway mentions how we will receive because of how good God is. Too often we make it about *our* reward!

The Gospel of Jesus! This says you have to die to your flesh!

> *"For if ye live after the flesh, ye shall die: but if ye through the Spirit do mortify the deeds of the body, ye shall live."*- Romans 8:13

MONEY ISN'T EVIL

"For the love of money is the root of all evil"

> *"For the love of money is the root of all evil: which while some coveted after, they have erred from the faith, and pierced themselves through with many sorrows."*-1 Timothy 6:10

The love of more or *(mammon)* is what caused Eve to partake of the fruit in the Garden of Eden. Adam and Eve were offered everything and chose the one thing that God said not to eat of. It was satan who tricked them into the need to have more and become their own God. This is the root of all evil!

HAVE YOU EVER WONDERED WHERE WE GOT OUR DOLLAR BILL? $$$$

Let's take a look at a story and learn when religion twisted health and prosperity into wealth and prosperity using the story of Moses in the wilderness and how he brought the Israelites out of captivity. They stopped trusting Moses on the way to the Red Sea and God did something very interesting. Let's read this in the book of Numbers.

> *"And the people spake against God, and against Moses, Wherefore have ye brought us up out of Egypt to die in the wilderness? for there is no bread, neither is there any water; and our soul loatheth this light bread."*-Numbers 21:5

So God does something here in V. 6 and 7

> *"And the Lord sent fiery serpents among the people, and they bit the people; and much people of Israel died. Therefore the people came to Moses, and said, We have sinned, for we have spoken against the Lord, and against thee; pray unto the Lord, that he take away the serpents from us. And Moses prayed for the people."*- Numbers 21:6,7

> *"And the Lord said unto Moses, Make thee a fiery serpent, and set it upon a pole: and it shall come to pass, that every one that is bitten, when he looketh upon it, shall live. And Moses made a serpent of brass, and put it upon a pole, and it*

came to pass, that if a serpent had bitten any man, when he beheld the serpent of brass, he lived."- Numbers 21:8,9

This is a very interesting reference to Jesus Christ before making his famous quote in John 3:16. He wrote in John 3:14,

*"And as Moses lifted up the serpent in the wilderness, even so must the Son of man be lifted up:"-*John 3:16

So the apostle John here is referencing the Old Testament in Numbers. Moses is told to lift up the brazen or (*judged*) serpent and He is drawing a parallel that the Act of Moses is foretelling Jesus being crucified. Let me outline this for you. Jesus is lifted up and becomes sin for us. He is (*judged*) so that we will be healed just like the people of Moses's day. He is saying He wanted the people to look up and see what our Saviour would have to do for them. (**Sidenote,**) I find it interesting when we get a snake bite, *antivenom* is used to heal us. *This is so remarkable!* I told you this to make one point.

Moses's staff represented health and prosperity. *Hence the snake around the pole.* We have twisted it into meaning *Wealth* and prosperity. Take a look at the dollar sign on your phone and then think of where it came from...absolutely amazing! This might be a good time to take a look at a verse that has been twisted drastically!

(KJV) Jeremiah 29:11 *"For I know the thoughts that I think toward you, saith the Lord, thoughts of peace, and not of evil, to give you an expected end." This verse says that God knows his own thoughts of us, peace and not of evil, to give you an expected end. He says here expected, meaning He knows what will happen and He knows what is expected, but He doesn't say what that end is.*

He just says it's not unexpected! Now we will move on to the NIV comparison."

(NIV) Jeremiah 29:11 *"For I know the plans I have for you," declares the Lord, "plans to prosper you and not to harm you, plans to give you hope and a future."*

Did you catch this in this text? It says, He plans to give us hope and a future..*this is entirely different! This version makes the gospel about us!* This is prosperity because it offends less people. *We now sell more Bibles!*

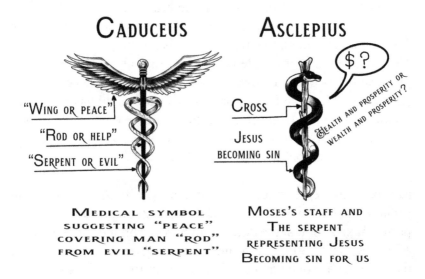

Medical symbol (Caduceus) on left, and (Asclepius) on right, used in the medical field.

666 CURRENCY AND THE MARKINGS

"And he causeth all, both small and great, rich and poor, free and bond, to receive a mark in their right hand, or in their foreheads:"-Revelation 13:16

We have all heard this scripture quoted by everyone. People have a way of applying knowledge without first diving into the source. This is my attempt at exposing this largely misunderstood subject. I can at least give you the resources to search for yourselves. I believe personally that the beast is obviously not some giant science fiction Godzilla most people so eloquently seem to mindlessly adopt.

This is another perfect example of how men have twisted the Bible to fit some superstitious fear based misunderstandings! This (666), has been called the *(Mark of the Beast)* which happens during the Rapture or the 7 year tribulation when God releases His wrath on earth. It is said, if people refuse to follow satan they will receive the mark upon their heads. Many people throughout the years have pinned this *"Beast"* identity to people such as *Adolph Hitler, the Pope, or different political leaders.* Lets not let man make fear control our belief systems!

RELIGION OF THE MARK OF THE BEAST

> *"Here is wisdom. Let him that hath understanding count the number of the beast: for it is the number of a man; and his number is Six hundred threescore and six."*-Revelation 13:18

Actually this number derives from the Greek *"Christos"* or the numerical value of *666*. If you take the numerical value of the first and last letters of this word and put a serpent in the middle. The numerical values add up to the *Pseudo* or *(Anti-Christ)*. Many people speak of *RFID* chips or (transponders) which are implanted under the skin for the use of machines or technology. (*This is the ultimate control of man.*) Another popular discussion is the use of the bar code you see on the back of any purchased products. Both of these are overlooking the fact that the scriptures refer to it being used as *(HIS number and not ours!) (All of this clearly has nothing to do with this passage of scripture.)*

> *"And that no man might buy or sell, save he that had the mark, or the name of the beast, or the number of his name."*- Revelation 13:17

So often we find ourselves a part of a conspiracy when we directly ignoring the Bible as the final authority. Religion has again taught us to just adopt other ideologies rather than looking for ourselves. The scripture says if you take on the pledge of his identity then you are bound by it! This reminds me of a*nother verse* in the Bible. This mark will clearly signify our allegiance to the anti-christ leadership.

> *"And Jesus answering said unto them, Render to Caesar the things that are Caesar's, and to God the things that are God's. And they marvelled at him."*-Mark 12:17

You may be wondering why I am bringing this verse up. Jesus is telling the people here to give to Caesar what is his. If your *political and financial* dedication is a man here, then this becomes the face of your identity. This becomes your god on earth.

> *"He that leadeth into captivity shall go into captivity: he that killeth with the sword must be killed with the sword. Here is the patience and the faith of the saints."*-Revelation 13:10

> *"And have ye not read this scripture; The stone which the builders rejected is become the head of the corner:"*

> *Vaticanus*

WHO IS ACTUALLY THE BEAST?

The beast's identity would more likely be found with a complete study of the Bible as a whole, rather than using a few customary religious things you might have heard. These 10 horns, and 7 heads with *10* crowns resembling a leopard of this so-called *"Beast"* of Revelation 13:1-2 are very obviously not a *(large animal.)* The book of Daniel sheds even more light on this subject.

> *"After this I saw in the night visions, and behold a fourth beast, dreadful and terrible, and strong exceedingly; and it had great iron teeth: it devoured and brake in pieces, and stamped the residue with the feet of it: and it was diverse from all the beasts that were before it; and it had ten horns."*- Daniel 7:7

> *"Then I would know the truth of the fourth beast, which was diverse from all the others, exceeding dreadful, whose teeth were of iron, and his nails of brass; which devoured, brake in pieces, and stamped the residue with his feet; And of the ten horns that were in his head, and of the other which came up, and before whom three fell; even of that horn that had eyes, and a mouth that spake very great things, whose look was more stout than his fellows. I beheld, and the same horn made war with the saints, and prevailed against them; Until the Ancient of days came, and judgment was given to the saints of the most High; and the time came that the saints possessed the kingdom. Thus he said, The fourth beast shall be the fourth kingdom upon earth, which shall be diverse from all kingdoms, and shall devour the whole earth, and shall tread it down, and break it in pieces. And the ten horns out of this kingdom are ten kings that shall arise: and another shall rise after them; and he shall be diverse from the first, and he shall subdue three kings. And he shall speak great words against the most High, and shall wear out the saints of the most High,*

43

and think to change times and laws: and they shall be given into his hand until a time and times and the dividing of time. But the judgment shall sit, and they shall take away his dominion, to consume and to destroy it unto the end. And the kingdom and dominion, and the greatness of the kingdom under the whole heaven, shall be given to the people of the saints of the most High, whose kingdom is an everlasting kingdom, and all dominions shall serve and obey him. "-
Daniel 7:19-27

Here's how I will close this section. Studying both the book of Daniel, as well as the volume of the Bible itself, you may come to a less *Science Fiction Thriller* based conclusion. The term *(beast)* refers to *two* related entities: The End times Empire. The 10 horns and 7 heads indicates that the beast will be a coalition of Nations that will eventually rise up and take dominion over the earth and take total control. As you read later in the book of Revelation, you will see a political leader that will wage war against God's people. It is more likely that the beast mentioned isn't the Anti-Christ himself. Here is another reference.

"Who opposeth and exalteth himself above all that is called God, or that is worshipped; so that he as God sitteth in the temple of God, shewing himself that he is God."-2 Thessalonians 2:4

"Let no man deceive you by any means: for that day shall not come, except there come a falling away first, and that man of sin be revealed, the son of perdition;"-2 Thessalonians 2:3

"I considered the horns, and, behold, there came up among them another little horn, before whom there were three of the first horns plucked up by the roots: and, behold, in this horn were eyes

like the eyes of man, and a mouth speaking great things."- Daniel 7:8

"And I saw the beast, and the kings of the earth, and their armies, gathered together to make war against him that sat on the horse, and against his army. And the beast was taken, and with him the false prophet that wrought miracles before him, with which he deceived them that had received the mark of the beast, and them that worshipped his image. These both were cast alive into a lake of fire burning with brimstone."-Revelation 19:19-20

"I beheld then because of the voice of the great words which the horn spake: I beheld even till the beast was slain, and his body destroyed, and given to the burning flame."-Daniel 7:11

ARE TATTOOS THE MARK OF THE BEAST? RELIGION AGAIN!

This concept fascinates me. Too many people appeal to common statements they hear and cherry pick their personal opinions, thus placing judgment on others when they themselves are full of sin. Let's assume tattoos are sinful. I would ask you if you have any piercing on your body. God makes it very clear that bodies represent God's new temple to house Jesus inside of us.

"Know ye not that ye are the temple of God, and that the Spirit of God dwelleth in you?"- 1 Corinthians 3:16

Religion gets so caught up in the details of who is right and who is wrong, when in reality, God is simply telling us that bodies are the new temple and to let the Holy Spirit (*the Other Comforter*) reveal Himself to you through the Word of God. This word *"tattoo"*

45

is found in the *NIV* and *NOT* in the *KJV Bible,* but can be found in other versions. Most religious people like to reference a verse in Leviticus 19:28

> *"Ye shall not make any cuttings in your flesh for the dead, nor print any marks upon you: I am the Lord."*- Leviticus 19:28

KEY WORD...*FOR THE DEAD*

Religious people routinely use this verse to condemn those with a marking on their body, yet the same person condemning, must have overlooked the two verses just before this, in V.26 and V.27.

> *"Ye shall not eat any thing with the blood: neither shall ye use enchantment, nor observe times. Ye shall not round the corners of your heads, neither shalt thou mar the corners of thy beard."*
> -Leviticus 19:26-27

Wait... should we not also cut off our beards or eat a yummy T-Bone steak? (*according to the Old Testament*) *Of course not!* This is a classic case of *"let me use scripture to condemn you, but not me!"* This was the Levitical law, written by Moses to the people of Israel. This was the dispensation or (*ERA*) of the law. Jesus wasn't born yet. Jesus would later appear in the book of Matthew and proclaim that He wasn't here to destroy the law, but fulfill it. The *Old Testament* was bound by law and the *New Testament* is by the grace of Jesus Christ.

> *"For the law was given by Moses, but grace and truth came by Jesus Christ."*-John 1:17

In conclusion, remember that Jesus was referring to Pegan practices, which included; not performing any ritualistic practices in remembrance of the dead or (*mourning.*) In closing maybe we should be focused on the underlying moral of God's message.

(What is his heart?) According to the Commandments we should make God our final authority and not man! Look what God says in the book of Isaiah!

> *"Can a woman forget her sucking child, that she should not have compassion on the son of her womb? yea, they may forget, yet will I not forget thee. Behold, I have graven thee upon the palms of my hands; thy walls are continually before me."*- Isaiah 49:15-16

Wait, What!? God has marked His hands with the names of Israel? Is it possible that religious people are cherry picking when they themselves break all commandments everyday? What does the entire scope of scripture say? If you read *Ephesians 2:15* you will notice that God brings Levitical Law to its end.

> *"Having abolished in his flesh the enmity, even the law of commandments contained in ordinances; for to make in himself of twain one new man, so making peace;"*-Ephesians 5:15

Jesus brought to end, Levitical laws like temple worship, sacrifices and food etc. We have been set free from these Levitical laws. It doesn't mean we are free to do whatever, but rather follow Jesus!

> *"For Christ is the end of the law for righteousness to every one that believeth."*-Romans 10:4

I want to make two things abundantly clear. If you are convicted that something you do will keep yourself or another from the glory of the Lord, my intent is not to offend or purposely misrepresent God. Let's not be martyrs. Let's read *Romans 14:13-23* carefully to gain better context.

> *"Let us not therefore judge one another any more: but judge this rather, that no man put*

a stumblingblock or an occasion to fall in his brother's way. I know, and am persuaded by the Lord Jesus, that there is nothing unclean of itself: but to him that esteemeth any thing to be unclean, to him it is unclean. But if thy brother be grieved with thy meat, now walkest thou not charitably. Destroy not him with thy meat, for whom Christ died. Let not then your good be evil spoken of: For the kingdom of God is not meat and drink; but righteousness, and peace, and joy in the Holy Ghost. For he that in these things serveth Christ is acceptable to God, and approved of men. Let us therefore follow after the things which make for peace, and things wherewith one may edify another. For meat destroy not the work of God. All things indeed are pure; but it is evil for that man who eateth with offence. It is good neither to eat flesh, nor to drink wine, nor any thing whereby thy brother stumbleth, or is offended, or is made weak. Hast thou faith? have it to thyself before God. Happy is he that condemneth not himself in that thing which he alloweth. And he that doubteth is damned if he eat, because he eateth not of faith: for whatsoever is not of faith is sin. "-Romans 14:13-23

Here again is another place where markings are mentioned on Jesus himself.

"And he hath on his vesture and on his thigh a name written, King Of Kings, And Lord Of Lords. "- Revelation 19:16

In closing, I will say this: Focus on the heart of God rather than the religion of man. This is why Jesus went to the cross in the first place.

"Thou hypocrite, first cast out the beam out of thine own eye; and then shalt thou see clearly to cast out the mote out of thy brother's eye."-
Matthew 7:5

The funny thing about judgment is like someone driving a car at night. They honk at the person heading toward them for having their bright headlights on, but pay no attention to the fact that their own headlights are set on high beams! They cannot see their own lights!

Chapter 5

THE BIG BANG?

EVOLUTION-THE BIG BANG!!

This could very well be my favorite part of this book. Lets first explore the Big Bang, as it is often called. I think the first thing that we need to do is understand how sound works! We do know that there is a phenomenon called a sonic boom: or according to the Webster Dictionary:

-Definition of sonic. 1: utilizing, produced by, or relating to sound waves sonic altimeter broadly : of or involving sound sonic pollution. 2 : having a frequency within the audibility range of the human ear —used of waves and vibrations. 3 : of, relating to, or being the speed of sound in air or about 761 miles per hour (1224 kilometers per hour) at sea level at 59°F (15°C)

I really enjoy the concept of this idea. Fast moving sound that separates still air from air that proceeds forth in a very fast way...*Hmm this reminds me of something else that I have read about!*

If Revelation 19:13 says that Jesus is the Word of God, and John 1:1 says,*"In the beginning was the Word and the Word was with God and the Word was God,"*

then based upon the Word or (*Jesus Christ*) in Revelation and the fact that John 1:1 saying the Word was God and it was with Him, then I can only draw one conclusion:

> *"And God <u>said</u>, Let there be light: and God divided the light from the darkness."*-Genesis 1:3

When God spoke the words, *"let there be light,"* His literal words came forth physically and manifested himself in *His spirit because His physical body* is not born until the book of Matthew! Here's the point. When God decided He would utter a sound (*from before the foundation of time*) he would make his breath itself, Jesus Christ! I would imagine at this time, there was no sound present, and nothing happened until His words came forth *instantly*! I could imagine this extremely intense sound (*that would have moved at such a rate of speed*) being *"Super Sonic!"* Oh wait, maybe there's your *Big Bang!*

Prepare yourself! This is going to get bumpy if you have any pre-conceived ideas about evolution. Again, I am asking you to take an unbiased look at what I am about to show you and let the Bible teach itself!

Evolution is *one* of satan's first lies. It is a religious belief taught with no validity whatsoever. So many false findings have been fabricated in our school systems and have all been debunked.

"SUPPOSABLY NOTHING EXPLODED AND MADE EVERYTHING"

I thought explosions destroyed things, not created them? <u>*Explosions cause death, not creation!*</u> This would be like going to a fancy art show and admiring the creators work of art and saying,*"wow"* this is a beautifully articulated explosion, and I want to compliment you

Mr. or Mrs. No one! Tell me, how did you form such intricate creations and design using colors, motion, creativity and light? *That explosion must have originally been a beautiful nano plasma at one time, right?* The truth is we have never seen new information added in a (*genome*) that has added to natural selection or adaptation, that has produced anything, *EVER!* Matter has never generated an information system, like (*gene pools.*)*"Of course this is ridiculous!" Everything created, has a creator! Everything we buy has an instruction manual!* Evolutionists would **have** to believe in millions of years because how else would you convince anyone into believing random matter just swirled around and went...*poof*...and became a human? You have to say millions of years so it becomes totally incomprehensible, which would cause the person to ignore logic and just think..hmm I suppose millions would explain it!

George Wald said it best in, *"**The Origin of Life**," Scientific American 191, no. 48* (*August 1954*) *"Time is in fact the hero of the plot...What we regarded as impossible on the basis of human experience is meaningless here. Given so much time, the "impossible" becomes possible, the possible probable, and the probable virtually certain! One has only to wait: time itself performs the miracles."* Time becomes the *god* of the evolutionists, yet The God of the Bible lives outside of time!

> *"All things were made by him; and without him was not any thing made that was made."*- John 1:3

This doesn't take a scientist or even a *third* grade understanding. We have become too scholarly and psychologized. We have it backwards. God prophesied the end from the beginning, so maybe the unbeliever of creation is right about evolution at least somewhat. I believe they will hear the explosion (*at the end*) from the beginning.

If the enemy can get you to disregard the book of Genesis and creation, then he can get you to discredit the rest of the Bible. Evolutionists and creationalist have two very different approaches to how they view the Bible. Evolutionists believe that everything was basically created by a giant explosion and then we just *"poofed"* into existence with beating hearts! It suggests that we're basically advanced results of cosmic seaweed. Basically in this religion, no real time can be nailed down so we use what is called *carbon dating*, which has proved to be inaccurate as well as *rock layer analysis*. A flood of monumental proportions could cause the great fossil records that have been found. We also suggest millions of years by default. I believe most people cannot comprehend this amount of time, so it seems to be a default that makes all of our genetic differences of the assumed *(evolution)* seem more believable.

CAVEMEN

The first thing you may think of is the *finch* made famous by *Mr. Darwin.* He studied extinct mammals fossils and their similarities. He basically assumed that since animals had similar features they must have morphed into one another. This is absolutely ridiculous for many reasons. Evolutionists assume that since we can compare animal structures to human structures, we assume they are similar and must have come from one another. This is silly. This just means that we have a common creator, and His name is God! All forms of human remains from *"millions of years ago,"* have been debunked. The phrase ***"millions of years"***is so incomprehensible in our human minds that it's a perfect (*default*) conclusion when there is no other way to explain evolution! (*if we say millions, then it must have happened, just because of millions!*) Evolutionalists love this word because it's big enough to somehow explain their lack of scientific proof!

Everything dies! How would something change if the old one died? How could certain animals survive during the between stages? An example of this is a giraffe. A giraffe has a certain function of blood circulation in its neck which prevents blood from rushing down its neck (*when moving its neck from 20 feet in the air) when eating.* When it would lower it's neck, It would simply pass out. If there was an *"in between evolutionary stage,"* then the animal in between would not function properly and be able to survive!

Here is a list of prehistoric humans that you may have heard of. *This list is made-up lies!*

Heidelberg Man-(*Heidelberg Man, named Homo heidelbergensis, was based on a single jawbone (known as the "Mauer Jaw") discovered near Heidelberg, Germany in 1907, by Daniel Hartmann.. It turned out to be Pig Jawbone! FAKE*

Nebraska Man-(*Considered a species of Ape.) Was considered the first 'higher primate' in North America. Discovered by (described by) Henry Fairfield Osborn in 1922, one piece of a tooth was found by rancher and geologist Harold Cook in Nebraska in 1917. It turned out to be the tooth of an extinct pig. FAKE*

Piltdown Man-(*Charles Dawson, an English lawyer and amateur geologist, found what appeared to be the fossilized fragments of a cranium, a jawbone, and other specimens in a gravel formation at Barkham Manor on Piltdown Common near Lewes in Sussex. This was discovered in 1912. FAKE.* This was the jawbone of a modern ape. It was a fraud and found and treated with iron salts.

PekingMan—(*Peking Man-Homo erectus pekinensis, formerly known by the junior synonym Sinanthropus pekinensis) is a group of fossil specimens of Homo erectus, dated from roughly 750,000 years ago, FAKE.* it was discovered in 1929–37 during excavations at Zhoukoudian (*Chou K'ou-tien*) near Beijing (*at the time spelled Peking),* China.- *Actually all of this evidence just DISAPPEARED!*

Neanderthal Man— (*Neanderthal, (Homo neanderthalensis, Homo sapiens neanderthalensis), also spelled Neandertal, member of a group of archaic humans who emerged at least 200,000 years ago during the Pleistocene Epoch (about 2.6 million to 11,700 years ago) and were replaced or assimilated by early modern human populations (Homo sapiens) between 35,000 and perhaps 24,000 years ago—**all fake!!** Actually this was found in a cave but it turned out to be a man suffering from arthritis! **Fake!***

Javaman -*(Java Man)* (Homo erectus erectus, formerly also Anthropopithecus erectus, Pithecanthropus erectus) is an early human fossil discovered in *1891 and 1892* on the island of Java *(Dutch East Indies, now part of Indonesia.)* Estimated to be between *700,000* and *1,000,000* years old, it was, at the time of its discovery, the oldest hominid fossils ever found, and it remains the type specimen for Homo erectus. Completel*y fake!* It turns out that there was concealed evidence. The teeth were from an orangutan. All of these made-up stories were taught in school and adopted as true and this is a very good example again of taking on a belief system and believing it. *It is religion!* Creationists believe that the Bible is very clear that we are born in six literal days and had one creator.

Evolution vs Creation

Genesis 1. One is religion and fabrication through default (*millions of years*) and the other is biblically defined through scripture. Evolution basically asserts that our planet is 4-7 billion years old.

The Evolution theory being taught in our schools violates the 1st Amendment and is:

> *"Congress shall make no law respecting an establishment of religion, or prohibiting the free exercise thereof; or abridging the freedom of speech, or of the press; or the right of the people peaceably to assemble, and to petition the Government for a redress of grievances."*

CARBON DATING SCIENTOLOGY & FOSSILS ?

Carbon dating and fossil recovery are extremely useful scientific studies that (***DO NOT***) prove evolution, which are taught in our public schools systems. The gatekeepers of the educational system are attempting to destroy the truth of creation! They actually only help to prove it.

We have been taught that the Grand Canyon was formed over *millions of years* to help provide a stronger case against creation. The Grand Canyon actually helps to *prove* the great flood! The topic of Carbon dating would (*in itself,*) take up a whole book, so I'll just give you (*in a nutshell*) an extremely primitive understanding of it in order to move on with my next point.

Carbon dating is known as the determination of the age or date of organic matter from the relative proportions of the carbon isotopes carbon-12 and carbon-14 that it contains. The ratio between them changes as radioactive carbon-14 decays and is not replaced by exchange with the atmosphere. Let me put this in layman's terms.

The problem with this form of "*age dating*" is that materials which absorb carbon and are tested, eventually stop absorbing

JESUS IS THE REVELATION

and essentially, *dry up* when the subject dies. *Ironically*, if evolutionists theories were actually true, and we took their word for it, then it would prove that carbon dating (***would be disregarded***!) ***Read this again until it hits you!*** What I just said would create circular reasoning, and would disprove carbon dating or evolution, but if either is wrong, then neither can carry any weight! Here's my point. These methods would have considerable, plausible and useful applications in *"young earth studies"* but in the case of evolution, this is impossible because patterns that are deemed constant are actually changing within themselves. We cannot measure accurately if something is *non-constant* (in the carbon dating theory.) I'll explain further.

If anything is studied, *(based upon a pattern or algorithm,)* such as a Rubik's Cube or a military inscription book, then the pattern would only be useful in calculating to a certain point. There would be a point in which we have no remaining pattern to observe. It would be at this point that we would have no idea of whether or not the pattern (*itself*) would change. Therefore we could not measure past the *original* pattern to **scientifically** observe ANYTHING! We have Scientific theory at best, and nothing to ***observe, measure or repeat. Science cannot observe eternity!*** but... ***I know who can! The God who lives outside of it. He lives outside of time itself!*** Carbon dating is futile, and proves ***nothing***! *(in the case of evolution!)* I know that science is highly regarded and useful, but there are way too many *"hypotheses"* relating to so many things that are not *"actually measurable,"* such as light years. In case you are wondering what light years have to do with this, I will gladly explain. If scientists can establish light year measurements, then they can use the same set of *theory* guidelines to establish distance and relativity, which would, in turn help to confirm their basis of evolutionary theory. These inaccurate measurements can act as rational comparisons to help date time and support their idea of moving particles of exploded space matter and use the distance it travels to make a (false) determination. If they can create a shred of doubt (*of a young earth*) and we take the bait, *(much like we do the National News,)* then if enough people are convinced and they put a scholarly stamp on it and teach it in your children's classroom, it will be trusted! I am all for science, just as long as we can *accurately observe, accurately measure and accurately repeat*. Once again...the problem is, *they* **cannot** *accurately measure at least two of the scientific laws!* I suppose I will give them one, ...(*observable.*)

My intention is *NOT* to destroy our love for science, but to observe it in a realistic, provable and factual way. Theories should be called theories. Creation can never, has never and will never be proven wrong! Now let's move on to something else observable.

FOSSILS

I love fossils! Fossils are a beautiful proof of our past. (*Our* **RECENT** *past.*) My sole purpose in mentioning fossils is because they are used to (*inaccurately*) attempt to disprove creation. Once again, the evidence used to do so is absolutely *not valid*. Let me explain another myth. Evolutionists use a worldview of fossil carbon dating that doesn't biblically or literally make any sense. Fossils typically form very quickly, and have been found all over the earth. Evolutionists love this fact until you mention the ones on mountain tops, (*which are above sea level.*) *What could possibly cause billions of dead things to be buried by receding water*? Take a look at Genesis *6-9* for the details. After the flood, animal carcasses would have spread everywhere. First of all, many of those"*old bones*" have been found with living red blood cells, which could not be present for more than a short time period.

Currently we can make *rock layers, petrified wood, gemstones and oil*, in a laboratory, in a matter of minutes, that look exactly the same as bones found by excavators, who use them in attempts to (***try***) to prove evolution. We can heat them up to about *400* degrees fahrenheit, using about *3500 lbs* of pressure to do so. The average ocean is about *12,000* feet deep, and would clearly be the perfect scenario in a global flood. The flood came from within the earth and from the sky. The flood of Genesis, is a perfect explanation of these *fossils!* The Grand Canyon provides so much information regarding the subject of fossils. Rock layers are found all the way up into the mountains as well! *This also points to a global flood!* Oddly enough the Grand Canyon displays *"rapidly"* deposited rock layers on the *(top.)* If erosion happens, *(according to evolution)* over millions of years, then how did large animals from entirely different regions get buried side by side? How would a few centimeters of sediment take thousands of years to develop the many layers without disturbing the carcuses? How could water slowly erode over millions of years, and then run uphill and drain out of the northern region of the Grand Canyon? *The answer is* **CREATION***, and a* **catastrophic flood***!* It's interesting to note that a twelve foot long fish was found with food still in its belly, which seems a bit odd to think that it wouldn't have decayed over millions of years. *We cannot preserve a ham sandwich for even seven days in our refrigerator.* **Fossils, carbon dating and rock layers** *"do not"* prove evolution!

LIGHT YEARS?

Light years are another fascinating study that attempts to pin creation to millions of years. Once again, this system of measurement is another *(supposed authority)* way of measuring the age of the earth, rather than just reading the Bible. This measurement claims to measure distance rather than time. *"Light year"* assumes time, but is defined by distance, yet it's distance is used to calculate time because of the distance of its relative objects. This is a tricky play on words. In either case, it *can* **not** measure the age of the earth! *Yes, I said it!* It cannot measure time! Light is known to travel *299,792,458 meters per second.* Science uses calculations of two points, *(with a little math equation)* and the time light takes to travel between the two. They would take distance divided by time to get the speed of light. The problem is we can only measure light speed by using reflective measurements. We can never use one direction only. We can never know how long light would have taken to hit a star, *(for example)* but we can measure when it returns, which gives us our measurement! The other problem is that even if this method worked, it would only be useful in measuring objects within our relative view in perspective. If this unit of measurement were plausible, (*using this method of distance measurement to prove a big bang and particle movement,*) it wouldn't be observable past the point of the stars that we can see. (For example,) We never know if the pattern of light travels at a specific speed (*definitively,*) other than theory. We can only demonstrate speculation at best! Light Years are interesting and useful, but prove nothing!

Einstein's quote says, "*is neither a supposition, nor a hypothesis about the physical nature of light, but a stipulation that I can make of my own free will to arrive at a definition of simultaneity.*" In conclusion, light years are very interesting measurements and useful (*as always,*) in the study of a *young earth* and prove creation! Evolution *once again* misses the mark!

SCIENTOLOGY

Scientology is a set of *pseudoscientific* beliefs and practices invented by American author *L. Ron Hubbard*, and an associated movement. It has been variously defined as a cult, a business or a new religious movement. Hubbard initially developed a set of ideas which he represented as a form of therapy, called Dianetics. The word "scio" comes from the Latin meaning "*knowing*" or "*inner knowledge.*" The Greek (*logos*) means "*word.*" I have heard some say that Scientology is the study of knowledge, but when I see the definition as "*inner knowledge*" of the word, it reminds me of a couple words spoken by satan, in the Garden.

> **"For God doth know that in the day ye eat thereof, then your eyes shall be opened, and ye shall be as gods, _knowing_ good and evil."**- Genesis 3:5

This is interesting to me. Before this point, it was clear that God's perfect plan was the Tree of Life, rather than the knowledge of sin.

RACE COLOR & KINDS?

There is only One race! God made the human race. *Jews and Gentiles.* Jews are descendants of the twelve tribes of Abraham and the Gentiles are everyone else! We are all of Adam's race, or the human race. There is a very simple thing called *Melanin. This is just skin pigmentation! That's all it is!* We've been killing each other for years over the color of skin pigment. This is just another way satan will get us to hate each other. God never once, mentions any biblical principles that deter, (*so called,*) *"interactial"* marriage because *interatial*, makes *no* sense at all, considering we are only one race! We are all ultimately related! Think about it! When you were a child, you didn't think *"man, I don't really want to play with little Bobby because he is white or black."* You didn't care! *Because you hadn't been taught to hate yet.* You were not old enough for satan to gain control of your mind!

Beginning in Genesis 1-11. All of the foundational information about life creation and marriage are founded. I've only found two definitive things that God seems to strictly say. Number one, He refuses to see one's outward appearance.

> *"But the Lord said unto Samuel, Look not on his countenance, or on the height of his stature; because I have refused him: for the Lord seeth not as man seeth; for man looketh on the outward appearance, but the Lord looketh on the heart."*- 1 Samuel 16:7

The second thing He says is *we are not to be unequally yoked.*

> *"Be ye not unequally yoked together with unbelievers: for what fellowship hath righteousness with unrighteousness? and what communion hath light with darkness?"*-2 Corinthians 6:14

The yoke was typically a wooden harness that was put across the neck of two "equally" powered Oxen. This yoke would keep them plowing in line with each other. They would have similar strength and would work well together. Jesus makes a reference to the yoke, in scripture;

> *"Thou shalt not plow with an ox and an ass together."*-Deuteronomy 22:10

The Ox is strong, smart, fast and obedient, whereas the donkey, *(ass) is weak, dumb, slow and rebelious.* These two creatures will <u>never</u> work well together. God is using this parallel to teach us that if we are an *(Ox for God,)* then we need to be yoked with another Ox. Even if the Ox is young it is still an Ox. The donkey will always hinder your advancement in the Kingdom of God, and will never work! *Don't worry, if you don't have another Ox, God will provide one for you.. Check this out in Matthew 11.*

> *V.28"Come unto me, all ye that labour and are heavy laden, and I will give you rest."*
>
> *V.29"Take my yoke upon you, and learn of me; for I am meek and lowly in heart: and ye shall find rest unto your souls."V.30"For my yoke is easy, and my burden is light."*- Matthew 11:28-30

HOW DID THEY FIT ON THE ARK?

When God created man He included genetic diversities within our genes. For example, God made two of each different kinds of species, collected them and placed them in the Ark. The Bible says the word *(kind.)*

> *"Of every clean beast thou shalt take to thee by sevens, the male and his female: and of beasts that are not clean by two, the male and his female."*- Genesis 7:2

"They, and every beast after his kind, and all the cattle after their kind, and every creeping thing that creepeth upon the earth after his kind, and every fowl after his kind, every bird of every sort."- Genesis 7:14

I'm not going to spend much time mentioning a *(they wouldn't fit)* myth. It was totally possible to fit all of the animals in the Ark. First of all, the birds of the air didn't need to enter the Ark, and animals under the water would also be excluded. This eliminates the majority of earth dwelling animals. *Yes, dinosaurs could have fit!* Why would God bring large, sick and old ones? They were most likely very small. People often wonder how so many different dogs, bears or alligators would have fit. If you were to observe the *kind* or *(family)* level, which is *canine*, rather than every single species that would be, *(after the flood.)* They would have developed over several hundred years. There would be *wolves, coyotes, wild dogs, bulldogs, collies,etc,* and all would derive from the *kind or Family,* which is *canine!* There would only need to be the "*canine,*" kind. This is very possible. People ask how dinosaurs could have fit on the Ark but if you do some research, you will find that *dinosaurs*, much like any other animals, have kingdom, Phylum, Class, Order and Family levels. The *(kind)* level of dinosaurs are *(T-Rex, Rapure, and Sauropods etc.)* All of these are all *(kind)* levels. It would seem sensible to think that God could have put young healthy versions of the dinosaur kinds on the Ark, which would only be the size of a sheep or pony. There are only about fifty or so dinosaur kinds in all and they would have easily fit on the Ark. There were likely about *1000-1400* kinds of all animals, at the family level of the animal kingdom, and they would have all fit very comfortably on the Ark!

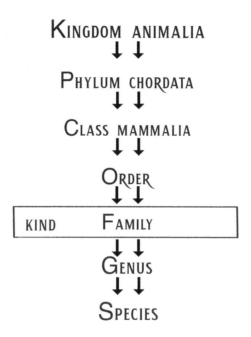

KINGDOM ANIMALIA
↓ ↓
PHYLUM CHORDATA
↓ ↓
CLASS MAMMALIA
↓ ↓
ORDER
↓ ↓

| KIND | FAMILY |

↓ ↓
GENUS
↓ ↓
SPECIES

The *(kind)* is considered the *(family)* level.

ARE PUREBRED ANIMALS BETTER?

I will provide a couple interesting diagrams that clearly explain why evolution is completely ridiculous! I want to make it clear that satan wants us to teach our children these lies in order to remove the idea of creation which completely removes the need for a creator! In this diagram, these original two cats, each carry both of the *(Long Hair, and Short Hair,)* or **(LS)** genes. Let's imagine they have kittens. These three new kittens would carry, (only) the two genes that were passed down from their parents. The only difference is that now, these kittens would grow up to be cats which received different variations of their *"parents"* genes. Here is an example. *(SS, SL, LL.)* As this pattern would repeat throughout hundreds of years, thousands or if not *millions* of variations could form from this process! Here's an example; *(SSL,SLS,LLL,LLSl)*, etc. These patterns could increase in many different variations. Over time you would see certain dominant traits survive in some regions and others, survive in other regions. The cats with longer haired genes, *(predominate,)* would eventually die off in desert environments, and short haired cats would no longer flourish in colder environments. Here's an example:

Long Hair Cold weather	Short Hair Warm weather
Maine Coon cat	*Abyssinian cat*
Scottish Fold cat.	*American Shorthair cat*
Siberian cat	*American Wirehair cat*
Norwegian Forest cat.	*Bengal cat*
Ragdoll cat	*Bombay cat*
Russian Blue Cat.	*British Shorthair*
Himalayan Cat	*Burmese cat*
Persian cat.	*Chartreux cat*

Evolutionists forgot *one* small detail about this whole process! There is **never** a time throughout this entire process that a **new** gene such as (*w,*) ever showed up! No new *DNA* information. There are only new species which are variations of the original copies. This is exactly the same with humans! Eventually weather and surroundings affect the environment for hundreds of years! We will notice hair change, eye color change, skin color change, and language change. We still never received new information called *evolution*, but we just have many variations of what already exists! If one creator created everything then there would obviously be evidence of the same creator in all things. Monkeys have similarities to humans, and dogs may have 4 legs, like cats. We both have hearts, and blood vessels and give birth. Evolution is ridiculous!

Long Hair, Short Hair, Create SS, LS, LL, but no new Information has been added to Genepool. The new combinations would include all different variations of Short Hair and long hair, but will never gain new original information.

You may have heard of dog breeding. Most people think of dog breeding as this amazing way of keeping a dog's breed pure. But what's really happening is they're mating closer genes with even closer genes causing more birth defects and in effect, unhealthy dogs. This would be the same as mating a mother with her son. The child would look like the parent but would have birth defects because of the dominant genes (*in a sense*) battling one another. Your everyday mutt would be the healthier dog! Evolution is a religion taught in our school systems that is an absolute lie.

Chapter 6

1 GOD IN 3 PERSONS

THE WORD OF GOD IS MANIFESTED

"In the beginning was the Word, and the Word was with God, and the Word was God."-John 1:1

"And the Word was made flesh, and dwelt among us, (and we beheld his glory, the glory as of the only begotten of the Father,) full of grace and truth."-John 1:14

These two terms have to make you ask the question, who is The Word? Who was with God and who is God! John 1:1 simply says the Word was all of these. Let's go find out where this *WORD* character is then! I want to draw your attention to the book of Revelation, in the New Testament. I am taking you there because in order to understand God, we must first read His *ENTIRE* Word.

"Then said I, Lo, I come (in the volume of the book it is written of me,) to do thy will, O God."-Hebrews 10:7

We now know that Jesus is in the entire volume of the book and if we are always reading, looking for Jesus, then will likely find Him on every page.

WHO IS THE WORD-JESUS CHRIST IS!!

As we move on to the book of Revelation, we will find our answer to who (*theWord*) actually is. Revelation Chapter *19* is describing this **White Horse** and **H**e is Jesus. As you read verses *11-16* you will discover an amazing thing.

> *"And I saw heaven opened, and behold a white horse; and he that sat upon him was called faithful and true, and in righteousness he doth judge and make war. His eyes were as a flame of fire, and on his head were many crowns; and he had a name written, that no man knew, but he himself. And he was clothed with a vesture dipped in blood: and his name is called The Word of God and the armies which were in heaven followed him upon white horses, clothed in fine linen, white and clean. And out of his mouth goeth a sharp sword, that with it he should smite the nations: and he shall rule them with a rod of iron: and he treadeth the winepress of the fierceness and wrath of Almighty God. And he hath on his vesture and on his thigh a name written, King Of Kings, And Lord Of Lords."*-Revelation 19:11-16

You will notice this white horse rider in V.13 has a vesture dipped in blood (The Slain Lamb) (Jesus) and in verse three, Jesus has a name written KING OF KINGS, And LORD OF LORDS. There are multiple references confirming Jesus Christ. V.15 even references Him as the two edged sword.

WHAT DID GOD SEE?

God saw what He said! In V.3 God says, *"Let there be light!"* When The Spirit of God moved over the water (*side note*): even the word *"let"* implies God's free will, even in His own creation. God is not a religious God. He is love! Then God said in V.6 the statement again , *"And God said, V.9,* And God ***said***", V.***11,14,20, 24, 26,*** all have the words *"God **said"*** and then you get to V.*31* and the bible says, *"**God saw.**"* You could ask this."What did He see?" The answer is simple. ***He saw what He said!*** He saw His Word manifested as He spoke It. It wasn't until He saw His Words, (*which is Jesus*) that anything happened. Things can exist around you but they are not manifested until you speak them. Jesus was the manifested Word of God at His creation! You will notice in V.4 of Genesis one, the first thing that God said was good, was the light He created. You may not have caught this. The light He created was ***not*** sunlight. That isn't until *day four*. God is obviously saying that light was good. There was darkness and then there was light. *"Remember that John the baptist bore witness of that Light!"*There is a message here.

> *"And the Word was made flesh, and dwelt among us, (and we beheld his glory, the glory as of the only begotten of the Father,) full of grace and truth. "*- John 1:14

In *John 1:1*, the Bible says in the beginning was the Word and we now know who the Word was referring to. *John 1:14* says that the Word or (*Jesus*) was made flesh on the earth, so we now know He was physically a man and the last part of V.14 says that His glory was physically witnessed, and was also known as the Son of God. This is amazing! He is the Son of God and walked the earth, but there is only one more question. Where did He begin? It was ***not*** in Bethlehem. Bethlehem is where He wrapped himself in flesh and wore His earth outfit. Jesus before becoming a man had an origin outside of time and it takes us right back to, *"The*

Beginning" which was just mentioned in *John 1:1.* Let's take a look at His amazing origin, shall we!

FROM THE BEGINNING

There is a familiar phrase in the 1st book of Genesis that sounds a lot like the book of John 1:1. *(In the beginning.)* This statement is also found in Genesis 1:1 ***"In the beginning God"***...As you read down to Genesis 1:26 ***"And God said, Let us make man in Our image,"*** Wait.. who is *Our*? Is someone with God, when He is speaking? The answer is *Yes*! John 1:1 said

*"In the beginning was the Word! The Word was with God, and The Word **was**, God! Jesus is the Word. Jesus was **with** God and **Jesus was God**.*

> ***"For there are three that bear record in heaven, the Father, the Word, and the Holy Ghost: and these three are one."***-1 John 5:7

These three are all correct in Genesis. God is so amazing! He even used His name *(Elohim,)* to express His *three separate identities.* He used the first *three* Lines of the Bible:

Genesis 1:1 *(In the beginning **God**,The (**Father**)*

Genesis 1:2 *(And the **Spirit** of God moved, (**Holy Spirit**)*

Genesis 1:3 *(And God **Said**, The (**Word**)*

> ***"All things were made by him; and without him was not any thing made that was made."***- John 1:3

God is saying that nothing was made without Him and He made All things!!

If we compare John1 V.1 and V.14 by their three separate sections, we see this.

John 1:1 <u>part 1</u> ***"In the beginning was the Word,"***

John 1:14 <u>part 1</u> ***"And the Word was made flesh,"***

John 1:1 <u>part 2</u> ***"and the Word was with God,"***

John 1:14 <u>part 2</u> ***"and dwelt among us,"***

John 1:1 <u>part 3-</u> ***"and the Word was God"***

John 1:14 <u>part 3</u> ***"and we beheld His glory,"***

The pattern is obvious! ***"In the beginning was the Word, and the Word was made flesh, and the Word was with God, and dwelt among us,***

And the Word was God, and we beheld His glory." *Jesus is the Manifested Word of the Living God.*

The point is, Jesus *is* the *Manifested Word of God,* and just like any good father, He has made Himself literally, available through His Word!

THE GODHEAD -TRIUNE GOD- or TRINITY?

Polytheo means *"Many" Gods" or poly.* Theo means *"**God**."* We have 1 God in *3* separate persons. He is *mon·o·the·istic, not 3 Gods or 1/3 each;* but He is one on His own as well as separately 3 individual persons in the same fashion. In the beginning was God and in three separate persons, and was also one. God spoke into existence the spirit of Jesus in the form of His Word, in Genesis 1:3. God manifested Himself in the being of Jesus Christ through the avenue His Holy Spirit. He would then wrap Himself in human flesh, *(in the womb of a woman,)* to dwell with man. He is the ***God man.*** He would become a spirit in a body that possesses a soul just like you and me. Jesus would live a sinless life unlike us, and would take on the sins of the world for the sake of you and me. He would be rejected by us and not even allowed a fair trial to defend

Himself. He was heaven sent and earth rejected and would die alone with even His Father God turning His head. He would open (*not*) his mouth, as He *gave* His life, and He would simply keep quiet and ask God to forgive us as we killed Him. This is exactly why my prayers are never, weak little, *(in your name prayers.)* or (in the lord's name.) **no way, <u>SAY HIS NAME!!</u>** *Would you hide your spouse from the world? Of course you wouldn't! If you sincerely loved her, would you tell your friends, "yeah, I'm married to that girl." no! You would say, "I love Katie or Sue or whoever!"* Jesus wants His name on our tongue in exactly the same way! *Love Him boldly!* I imagine God saying to us, *"Hey bride of mine, I've allowed an epidemic or a snow day to allow you to make time with me."* I believe He used our pain to advance His kingdom. We're so often unaware of His unimaginable love for us. He's courting us, and wants us to take Him seriously and start dating to marry! *You figure that one out on your own. Stop fooling around with being a small cross christian, and make a commitment!*

> *"For there are three that bear record in heaven, the Father, the Word, and the Holy Ghost: and these three are one."*-1 John 5:7

The Spirit and *The Word* **cannot** be separated! *Ever*! Religious denominations often claim that you can have one but not the other. If I were to claim to have an anointing of the Holy Spirit, and the Word does not align up with it, then I am a liar and I am to be completely ignored. Some versions, as I have mentioned elsewhere, have omitted this verse or in other cases, changed the words. *"These three are one" to "These are in agreement"* One means one, and agreement means *they agree*, but have nothing to do with **one**. Once again we have people altering God's Word to make other people happy or to sell more Bibles. God's original Word was to glorify Him alone! God will always reveal false prophets to us.

It may be hard for us to comprehend that God is one hundred percent God and one hundred percent man and one hundred percent

Holy Spirit but let me tell you this. Just because we cannot under-stand how He is one and also three separate persons doesn't make it illogical. This simply means we don't yet have a full comprehension of how He is Omnipresent (*everywhere at once*) or Omnipotent (with unlimited *power.*) God lives outside of the time He created so we cannot explain His dimension. This means we cannot possibly imagine it but we can trust His Words based upon the fact that He created our physical existence and placed us within His time realm. We can trust that God must have no bound-aries of His unlimited presence. This would mean He could easily be God as well as any other simultaneous existence if He wished. Simply put…we are three dimensional beings that are limited to our own knowledge of physics and time and we could in no way understand God's physical, spiritual or natural ways because He is God! God could manifest in 3, 5 or even 11 different dimensions or realms or times if He chose to!

There are **THREE** *who's* and **ONE** *what* !

"Within the one being, is God"
"There are three co equal and co-eternal persons"
"Father-Son-Holy Spirit"

"And Jesus, when he was baptized, went up straightway out of the water: and, lo, the heavens were opened unto him, and he saw the Spirit of God descending like a dove, and lighting upon him:"-Matthew 3:16

"For in him dwelleth all the fulness of the Godhead bodily."-Colossians 2:8

Jesus saw the Spirit of God or *Holy Spirit*. The Father and the Son are having an interaction.

THREE EXAMPLES OF 1 JOHN 5:7

TRI-UNE (3 & 1)
TRINITY (3 IN 1)
GOD IS 1 AND 3 INDIVIDUALLY
GOD IS TRI-UNE

"God is 100 Percent God, and 100 Percent Man. He is not just 3 parts, or 33 ⅓ each. God is 1 as well as 3 in entirely separate Persons"

Note:

>*"But if ye be led of the Spirit, ye are not under the law."*-Galatians 5:18

Why not leave all of the inspired Words of God the way they were originally printed?

You read this same verse in the *NIV* Bible, and it reads this *"For there are three that <u>testify</u>"* V. 8 *"the Spirit, the water and the blood; and the three are <u>in agreement.</u>"*

KJV VS NIV COMPARISON

>*"For there are three that testify: the spirit, the water and the blood; and these three are in agreement."*-NIV–1 John 5:7,8

"For there are three that bear record in heaven: the Father, the Word, and the Holy Ghost: and these three are one."-KJV -1 John 5:7,8

Wait wait wait! These *three* are *in agreement and* these three *are one,* have *entirely* different meanings! Some might say,"Oh well, these *three* are one, means the same thing as these *three* are in agreement. The word *One* here in *G1520 of the Strong Concordance* means (*literally*) ***ONE***. It doesn't mean, *"they are **as** one,"*or as if to say they agree as one. This is ***not*** the same. As you can see, the integrity of the Word of God, has been compromised here. *"Father"* means ***"God,"*** *"the Word Means"Jesus,"* Rev 19:13, and the *Holy Ghost."* KJV says that they *All* bear record, or testify in heaven and that they are one. One literally means all the same beings, or God, but all independently three separate persons. I often hear defense from different theologians that *"it was not supposed to originally be in the Bible."* This sounds like religion to me! Isn't it interesting that when a verse in the Bible interferes with someone's personal belief systems, we always seem to make changes to make it fit us!

Chapter 7

THE MYSTERY OF HEBREW

KING JAMES IS NOT "ARCHAIC"

P lease look in the original Hebrew language, which was Jesus's language. We read our Bible in Western English and probably in most cases, assume since we are reading an English Bible here in the US, that we must be right! Actually the Bible has no reference to the United States whatsoever. We as a western culture have decided since we don't use old *"archaic words"* that our current customs and languages *"must" be* correct. We also believe that the Bible needs to be translated so it relates to us now... *wrong*! How would you begin learning about your grandparents if you just expected them to learn how we do things? *You wouldn't*! You would first start by spending time with them, and learning their beginnings. (much like our Bible) when the times were much better and probably more accurate. In 1611 when the *King James bible* was printed, it was not a version and was written in proper English. They did not talk like, *"hello thou, and how art thou today."* Those archaic pronouns and prefixes were added with a direct purpose in mind. The King James Bible was written in what is called Middle English. God interjected these so-called *"archaic"* words with a purpose! Every single Word in the Canon of our KJV was placed specifically there by design. It was all for us but not necessarily written to us.

THEE, THY AND THOU, YE RELIGION SAYS *"CHANGE IT TO FIT US!"*

Did you know that the word "Thou with a *"T"* specifically references a singular individual and never references more than one!

Example: In the book of *John 3:1-8*, Jesus explained to the religious leader, *(Nicodemus)* how to be *Born Again,* and Jesus goes on to explain in *John 3:5, "Jesus answered,* **Verily, verily, I say unto (thee), Except a man be born of water and of the Spirit, he cannot enter into the kingdom of God."**-John 3:5

Here we notice **thee** and it is a direct statement to Nicodemus.

Jesus then goes on to say in John 3:7 *"**Marvel not that I said unto (thee,) Ye must be born again."**-*John 3:7

Here we see Jesus use the Word *(Ye)*. *Ye* refers to *(all)* of you or all in the group."

The point I'm making is that Jesus is talking to Nicodemus specifically using *(thee)* and says that *(Ye)* or everyone listening must be born again! Jesus is telling one man that all men need to be born again. This use of *(thee and Ye)* are very imperative when making the point when Jesus was speaking. If these Words were left out, then you *(the reader)* and I would miss the entire context of the verse, or more specifically, we have left the entire Bible up to interpretation and speculation. These words are not archaic, they are in every modern dictionary. With a small amount of effort and research, everything can be easily defined. We often take the lazy road and try to either read over the Word or assume it's unimportant.

Here is a short and simple list to explain that these words simply express singular or plural usage as well as tense usage, which was much more accurate than today's modern day English.

(SINGULAR)

(*Thou*)=you when the subject Ex. *"thou liketh my car"*

(*Thee*)=you when the object Ex. *"My car liketh thee"*

(*Thy*)=your possessive form of you. Ex *"Thy car well serves thee"*

(*Thine*)=your possessive form of you. Typically used before a noun. *"Thine car is thine"*

(PLURAL)

(*Ye, you and your*) a Group!

The reason I have gone to so much work to point out these grammatical facts is that so often religion says, "Oh that Bible is so archaic and hard to read and what they are really saying is, *"we need to update it and make a modern version"* and what they are really doing is changing truth to make it fit our new truth. The problem is that truth is *not* relative! So often you think of new translations such as *NIV, NASB* or *ESV* etc; and you hear," as long as we get the Word and the gospel, what's the big deal?" I said earlier, in the book of Revelation, not *one single* word of the Bible should be altered.

> *"For I testify unto every man that heareth the words of the prophecy of this book, If any man shall add unto these things, God shall add unto him the plagues that are written in this book:"*-Revelation 22:18

WHY SPEAK IN PARABLES?

There are biblical signatures in the Word of God, that are very similar to how you and I would sign our name. My closest friends would know if they saw my writing, because they have spent so much time getting to know me. It's a relationship, not a religion. In the book of Matthew chapter 13, Jesus is speaking to His disciples in parables, and explaining how He must speak in parables, because no one is listening to Him.

> *"And the disciples came, and said unto him, Why speakest thou unto them in parables? He answered and said unto them, Because it is given unto you to know the mysteries of the kingdom of heaven, but to them it is not given. For whosoever hath, to him shall be given, and he shall have more abundance: but whosoever hath not, from him shall be taken away even that he hath. Therefore speak I to them in parables: because they seeing see not; and hearing they hear not, neither do they understand. And in them is fulfilled the prophecy of Esaias, which saith, By hearing ye shall hear, and shall not understand; and seeing ye shall see, and shall not perceive: For this people's heart is waxed gross, and their ears are dull of hearing, and their eyes they have closed; lest at any time they should see with their eyes and hear with their ears, and should understand with their heart, and should be converted, and I should heal them. But blessed are your eyes, for they see: and your ears, for they hear. For verily I say unto you, That many prophets and righteous men have desired to see those things which ye see, and have not seen them; and to hear those things which ye hear, and have not heard them."*-Matthew 13:10-17

JESUS CHRIST IS THE ALEPH TAV

> Philipians 2:6 *"Who, being in the form of God, thought it not robbery to be equal with God:"*

WHAT IS THE TITTLE ?

Let's explore these two words. You might normally think of the jot and tittle in our English Bible as the "dotting of the *i* or the crossing of the *T*," but actually the *"jot,"* is the Hebrew letter for the word *"Yod"*, which is the smallest of the Hebrew alphabet. The *tittle* in our Bible is actually the smallest little mark, crown, or apex on *eight* of the Hebrew letters. The tittle is so small, that you may never even notice it. The *tittle* has profound meanings in word pronunciations. This is similar to vowels in our language. They are very important and cannot be overlooked in order to understand the language. The bible says in Matthew…

> *"For verily I say to you, Till heaven and earth pass, one jot or one tittle shall in no wise pass from the law, till all be fulfilled."*- Matthew 5:18

Please let me explain. The Hebrew alphabet was the first complete language known to man. There are *22* letters that were originally a pictograph. The smaller of the letters was the *yod*. The smallest little mark above *8* of the Hebrew pictographs was a *tittle*. It was symbolized by a little crown or an apex at the top. This was a very little mark almost overlooked by most people. *Psalms 119* in most King James Bibles, actually have the Hebrew letters symbolized above them. You may be wondering why am I bringing this up? Here's the answer that God is telling us clearly.

> *"Search the scriptures; for in them ye think ye have eternal life: and they are they which testify of me."*- John 5:39

He is saying, *"Religious person who knows so much,"* please look for Jesus in this book, rather than religion. Stop carrying the Bible around thinking you know me. Go into every page or every *Yod and tittle,* looking for a relationship with Me. Instead of being a scholarly, well read, and religious person and spend more time with me! God is telling us that not a *"Jot"(Yod)* or *tittle,* will be overlooked. Not even one word, or even one little letter, will be unimportant without specific purpose and it was put there by design!

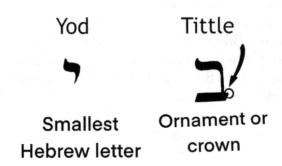

The **Yod** is the smallest of Hebrew alphabet, and the **Tittle** is the smallest mark on 8 of the Hebrew alphabet. This could be compared to the dotting of the **i** & the crossing of the **t**."

Often, we go into God's Word, expecting to find words to fit our specific belief systems. We'll cherry pick whichever part makes us feel better. The danger associated with contextual criticism, is that when we decide to apply our own religion to what we heard, or something someone said, it ultimately becomes a different version of the original truth. Truth is never relative! There is a baseline. It's called *Jesus!*

If two people are looking at a compass that is facing due north, and one man says, *"well my truth is due south"* and the other person says, *"my truth is due west,"* who is right? *The compass is!* What is our moral compass? I think a better question is *Who?* **"Jesus Christ is!!"** There is no truth apart from Him. Religion is the opinion, and it is *not relevant.* His Word is relevant!

My point is, religion and misrepresentation of scripture lands a death blow to Christianity! New christians and non believers hear and read things that put a sour taste in their mouths. My goal is to wet the tongue, and positively convict the mind of believers and nonbelievers towards scripture. The Bible is not written for the *overeducated, self proclaimed, deep thinking scholar. The Bible is written for everyone.* Wicca comes from the word *"wicker,"* *which means, "to twist."* If you look back in the first book of the Old Testament, it reads…

> **"And the Lord God commanded the man, saying, Of every tree of the garden thou mayest freely eat"**- *Genesis 2:16,*

> **"But of the tree of knowledge of good and evil, thou shalt (not) eat of it: for in the day that thou eatest thereof thou shalt surely die."**-Genesis 2:17

As we read further into Genesis *Chapter three,*

we see Eve confronted by Satan or *"the serpent"* and he proceeds to trick her. The Bible says he was more *"subtle"* than any beast of the field. *Wait, more subtle? Satan was sneaky and decided to change just*"One Little Itty Bitty Word!"

> **"And the serpent said unto the woman, Ye shall (not,) surely die"**-Genesis 3:4…

*There it is,the first lie ever! (**not**, is just <u>one</u> little word.) How can one little word matter in the Bible as long as the Gospel is there, right?* **wrong!** This is where the lie began, from the father of all lies!

> **"Ye are of the father of the devil, and the lusts of your father ye will do. He was a murderer from the beginning, and abode not in the truth, because there is no truth in him. When he speaketh a lie, he speaketh of his own: and for he is a liar, and the father of it!"**- John 8:44

This is how it all started. Satan altered the truth with one word. God made His purpose very clear on the earth, and made it known that He comes in the volume of the book, from cover to cover.

> *"Then said I, Lo, I come (in the volume of the book it is written of me,) to do thy will, O God."*-
> Hebrews 10:7

The lie started in the garden but God always prioritizes love first!

JESUS- THE ALPHA & THE OMEGA?

This chapter has one purpose. Initially I've stated why I believe the Bible and how the Bible came to us, as well as how satan can twist the words and letters just as he did in the Garden of Eden. I have given you information on how we can trust the Bible that we have entrusted and read. I think it's time to show you how intelligently God has formed His Word into an integrated message system, and communicated to us through The Word in a way that it is impossible to deny. The prophecy of Jesus occurred over a thousand years before his birth. Very specific details of his birth, as well his family lineage have been documented. As we keep reading the Bible, we see more bread crumbs along the way. There are *seven* times more prophecies recorded about Jesus's resurrection by eyewitnesses, than of his life beforehand!

Hopefully by now, you've seen something amazing and realize that Jesus Christ is in every single word, poem, song and letter of the *KJV* Bible. Even if we removed every page, and left only two, His fingerprints would still be preserved.

ALEPH OR ALEF-TAV OR TAU

Hebrew is an ancient pictogram language that is not phonetic like ours. It's a *twenty two* letter language made up of ancient pictures. Each letter has a number and picture associated with it that can be arranged in different forms to create picture words. There is no other language even remotely this amazing! Jesus spoke Hebrew. This is God's first complete language ever known to man. Most of the Old Testament was written in this language and the letters translated into Greek, which is a very specific language. The first letter of the Hebrew language is the (*Aleph or Alef.*) The Aleph is represented by an Ox head and it means *1, God, Strength* or *Service* or *Servant*. The last number of the Hebrew pictograph is the *Tav or Tau,* which is represented by two sticks placed over one another in the shape of a cross, which means a *Mark, destination* or a *Covenant*. The *Tav* also represents the number *400*, pictured here in the diagram below. These symbols are placed here together in the first line of the Hebrew Bible. When you combine these two letters together, which normally doesn't spell a word, you get "*AlephTav.*" What is Aleph Tav?

GREEK 1ST & LAST
LETTERS

ALPHA OMEGA

SAME AS ALEPH
& TAV TRANSLATED
FROM HEBREW

*The **Alpha** and **Omega**, are the first and last letters of the greek alphabet*

*The **Aleph** and **Tav**, are the first and last letters of the oldest Hebrew alphabet*

Aleph	*(The **Strong Servant**)(The OX)(God)(#1)*	*(**Jesus**)*
Tav	*…(**Destination**) (**Mark**) (**Covenant**)(400)*	*(**Cross**)*

"STRONG SERVANT, SERVING A MARK OR DESTINATION"

Jesus makes this statement in the book of Matthew.

> *"For verily I say unto you, Till heaven and earth pass, one **jot or one tittle** shall in no wise pass from the law, till all be fulfilled."*- Matthew 5:18

"Who, being in the form of God, thought it not robbery to be equal with God:"-Philippians 2:6

The point I am making is that Jesus says His words and letters from the beginning to the end of the Bible (*Genesis to Revelation,*) will never go away! Not one mark or letter can be overlooked, or ignored without a purpose being fulfilled! In the Authorized King James Bible, you will notice something in the book of *Psalms, chapter 119.* Every eighth verse begins another one of each of the Hebrew alphabet letters. If you look carefully in *Psalms 119:1-8* just before these *eight* verses, is the *Aleph* Symbol (*in Hebrew.*) Then again just before verses 9-16, you will notice the second letter of Hebrew *(Beth,)* and again you see the third letter of Hebrew *(Daleth,)* followed by verses 25-32. And so on and so forth. This follows the same pattern throughout all twenty two letters of the Hebrew alphabet and the pattern never changes. They all have eight verses exactly after each one of them until you get the last letter, (***Tau or Tav.***) It just so happens that the *number eight,* in scripture means, *"New beginnings."* You cannot tell me that a man just wrote this on his own and then unknown to him, stuck the forged (*precious*) TORAH writings right back into the hands of the Jewish Rabbi's. *I don't think so!* This is just another way God has wrapped His spirit up in prophecy to be discovered through His words. I added this information with the purpose of building your faith. This particular section of my book has no religious attention, but it does help to reinforce why we can trust the Word of God. I don't have time to go any deeper, but there is much more discovery to be made!

Jesus is saying that I am not only the words, but the letters that make up My Word!

"In the beginning was the Word, and the Word was with God, and the Word was God."-John 1:1

Jesus makes another statement that He is the Alpha and Omega, so let's take a deeper look at this.

"I am Alpha and Omega, the beginning and the end, the first and the last."- Revelation 22:13

"And he said unto me, It is done. I am <u>Alpha and Omega</u>, the beginning and the end. I will give unto him that is athirst of the fountain of the water of life freely."-Revelation 21:6

"<u>I am Alpha and Omega</u>, the beginning and the ending, saith the Lord, which is, and which was, and which is to come, the Almighty."- Revelation 1:8

"And when I saw him, I fell at his feet as dead. And he laid his right hand upon me, saying unto me, Fear not; <u>I am the first and the last:</u>"-Revelation 1:17

"Thus saith the Lord the King of Israel, and his redeemer the Lord of hosts; <u>I am the first, and I am the last;</u> and beside me there is no God."- Isaiah 44:6

"Hearken unto me, O Jacob and Israel, my called; I am he; <u>I am the first, I also am the last."</u>- Isaiah 48:12

*(Hint)**(Strong servant)***

It's interesting that Jesus was asking His parents quite literally:

"Wouldn't I be doing my Fathers work? If you knew that I was the Son of God? *"Wouldn't I be doing my Fathers Work?"*

"Wouldn't I be on an assignment?"

"Wouldn't God be at Church? From the cross, Jesus said,

"It is Finished" or **Tetelestai,** *(this is to say that)* *"a battle has been won!"*

Jesus is found in the temple and utters His first words in the book of Luke!

> *"And He said unto them, How is it that ye sought me? wist ye not that I must be about my Father's business?"*-Luke 2:49

"IN THE BEGINNING "BARASHETH"

This next diagram shows the very first line of the Bible in Genesis 1:1. Reading right to left, within one word you notice something very fascinating. Remember that I told you that Hebrew is a picture language. Below is a diagram showing the meaning of each letter of the First word. ***"Barahith."***

Each letter has a specific meaning *"just within the first word of the Bible"* each individual letter spells out a very important message. In the diagram below you will see the first line of the Hebrew Bible that reads, *"In the beginning created God."* The Hebrew language reads right to left. In our western culture we tend to believe that left to right is correct. Just like typical religious views, we are dead wrong! Hebrew is God's language, and it was established right to left. Leave it to satan to make even our language backwards in the US. You will notice that in the middle of these seven words that make the verse, you will see the Aleph and the Tav letters. Here's the funny thing. If you asked a Hebrew speaking native what they spelled, they would have no idea, because it doesn't even spell a word. The letters are just sitting there with no purpose...Or is there?

7	6	5	4	3	2	1
הָאָרֶץ	וְאֵת	הַשָּׁמַיִם	אֵת	אֱלֹהִים	בָּרָא	בְּרֵאשִׁית
Ha'aretz	V'et	Ha'shamayim	Et	Elohim	Bara	Bereshith
The earth	And	The heaven	-	God	Created	In the beginning

Hebrew reads right to left. Each letter has a number associated with it

This is the first line of the Hebrew Bible (right to left)

In the Beginning (בראשית)

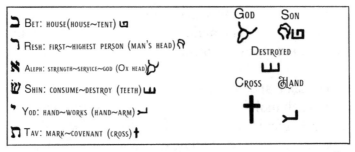

Bet: house(house~tent)
Resh: first~highest person (man's head)
Aleph: strength~service~god (Ox head)
Shin: consume~destroy (teeth)
Yod: hand~works (hand~arm)
Tav: mark~covenant (cross)

God   Son
Destroyed
Cross   Hand

"Son of God is destroyed by his own hand"

God put the message of the cross in the first line of the Bible

The first word of the Bible (*in Hebrew*) clearly says that *"The Son of God is destroyed,"(willingly,)* by his own hand, at the cross!" Unbelievable!

> *"**Who, being in the form of God, thought it not robbery to be equal with God:**"*-Philippians 2:6

THE MYSTERY OF HEBREW

LOOK FOR THE PATTERNS

The Bible is written with the intent that we would do a little digging for ourselves. God is using His language to identify His son Jesus Christ. God waited until the fortieth book of the Bible, which is the first book of the New Testament, to reveal His Son. He decides in this chapter to wrap Himself in flesh. Jesus didn't originate in Bethlehem. He was created before the foundation of time, and He uses numbers to express biblical principals like the number forty.

It's interesting that the Old Testament has *39* books, and the new has *27* because fulfillment of prophecy cannot happen until Jesus shows up on the scene, in the book of Matthew, (*which is the 40th book.*) Moses was in the wilderness 40 years. The Israelites were in captivity for 400 years. 40 different Bible authors, 40 days and 40 nights in the Ark at sea, 4 directions (*North East West South*) 4 seasons, 4th commandment, 4 rivers in creation. This list goes on and on. You will find hundreds and hundreds of the uses of the number *7* in the Bible. The number 7 means, *"Completion." 7 days for example.* I am trying to show that God has put so many patterns throughout His Word, and not even a super computer could not have planned out all of the hidden messages (*within messages*) that are all entirely integrated throughout every single letter of the Bible!

LOOK FOR THE PARABLES

> *"And the disciples came, and said unto him, Why speakest thou unto them in parables? He answered and said unto them, Because it is given unto you to know the mysteries of the kingdom of heaven, but to them it is not given. For whosoever hath, to him shall be given, and he shall have more abundance: but whosoever hath not, from him shall be taken away even that he hath. Therefore speak I to them in parables: because*

they seeing see not; and hearing they hear not, neither do they understand. And in them is fulfilled the prophecy of Esaias, which saith, By hearing ye shall hear, and shall not understand; and seeing ye shall see, and shall not perceive: For this people's heart is waxed gross, and their ears are dull of hearing, and their eyes they have closed; lest at any time they should see with their eyes and hear with their ears, and should understand with their heart, and should be converted, and I should heal them. But blessed are your eyes, for they see: and your ears, for they hear. For verily I say unto you, That many prophets and righteous men have desired to see those things which ye see, and have not seen them; and to hear those things which ye hear, and have not heard them."-Matthew 13:10-17

HIDDEN MESSAGES WITH THE GENEALOGIES

The lineage of Adam and Eve will further be explained in the next section of this book. You'll be shocked to discover how their seed would carry on through the generations of Adam and carry down to the birth of Noah, in Genesis chapter five. Most people would agree that *"begot, begot, begot, begot, would appear to be extremely boring!"* The original language of Hebrew will reveal something that will interest and surprise you. God never writes anything without a purpose! *Nothing is boring*!

> *"So shall my word be that goeth forth out of my mouth: it shall not return unto me void, but it shall accomplish that which I please, and it shall prosper in the thing whereto I sent it."*-Isaiah 55:11

The genealogies listed in Genesis 5 have a specific purpose of redemption and they mark the flood that I will talk about. The book of Genesis chapter *5* lists *10* generations starting with Adam and ending with Noah. The hidden truth within this chapter is mind blowing. When you read the passages between V.1 and 32 of Genesis 5, you will see a list of these 10 names. I will put their original Hebrew names and meanings next to them. *This gene-alogy is not translated in our English Bible.*

ADAM	(930)	.Man(is)	Mankind (Male and Female)
SETH	(912)	Appointed	Appointed lineage to Jesus(Able killed)
ENOSH	(905)	Mortal (Wound)	or incurable wound
(C) KAINAN	(910)	Sorrow;(Elergy)	sorrow or sadness(Pun)
MAHALALEL	(895)	The Blessed God	The blessed or praised God.
JARED	(962)	Shall Come Down	verb- "may mean things that fell"
ENOCH	(365)	Teaching	(God took him)(1st prophecy of Jesus)(with God)
METHUSELAH	(969)	His Death Shall Bring.	(His death would identify the flood)
LAMECH	(777)	The Despairing	(To Lamech or of Cain)
NOAH	(950)	Comfort, Rest	(Rest or cease to labor)

Let's read this in its literal sense. *"Man is appointed mortal sorrow, but the blessed God shall come down teaching that His death shall bring the despairing comfort, and rest!"*

This is a complete summary of the Christian Gospel, hidden within the text. There is no conceivable way that this could have been snuck into the cherished Jewish Torah in some hidden way. *It wouldn't happen!* This is just another amazing proof that God's Word was preserved! The late Mr. Chuck Missler said it best:

"The New Testament is in the Old Testament concealed and the Old Testament is in the New Testament revealed!"

THE GOOD SAMARITAN ETC.

There are so many amazing spiritual parallels in the canon of the Bible. I don't have time to even touch the surface, but two that I want to mention briefly will build your faith beyond belief! Listen to the story of the Good Samaritan, mentioned in the book of Luke 10:25-37. *Check this out!* Jesus is talking to a lawyer, and the man asks how to inherit eternal life. Jesus tells the man to love his neighbor and the man was less concerned about *(just loving)* rather than *(who)* he should love, and Jesus explained that man should love everyone! Jesus uses a spiritual principle that expresses how we are to love another. Let's explore the *deeper* underlying message!

> *"And, behold, a certain lawyer stood up, and tempted him, saying, Master, what shall I do to inherit eternal life?"*-Luke 10:25

Jesus goes on to tell the story of a *"certain man."*

> *V.30 "And Jesus answering said, A certain man went down from Jerusalem to Jericho, and fell among thieves, which stripped him of his raiment, and wounded him, and departed, leaving him half dead. V.31 And by chance there came down a certain priest that way: and when he saw him, he passed by on the other side. V.32 And likewise a Levite, when he was at the place, came and looked on him, and passed by on the other side. V.33 But a certain Samaritan, as he journeyed, came where he was: and when he saw him, he had compassion on him, V.34 And went to him, and bound up his wounds, pouring in oil and wine, and set him on his own beast, and brought him to an inn, and took care of him. V.35 And on the morrow when he departed, he took out two pence, and gave them to the host, and said*

> *unto him, Take care of him; and whatsoever thou*
> *spendest more, when I come again, I will repay*
> *thee. V.36 Which now of these three, thinkest*
> *thou, was neighbour unto him that fell among*
> *the thieves? V.37 And he said, He that shewed*
> *mercy on him. Then said Jesus unto him, Go, and*
> *do thou likewise."*-Luke 10:30-37

Let's see this story in a new way!

V.30 says, "A *certain man* went *down*." The Bible always uses the word *down* to represent someone *fallen* or someone *losing their way*. The Bible says (*down from*,) Jerusalem. The man left "*a Holy Place,*" and went *Down* to a *fallen* place. This sounds a lot like you and me. *V.31* says that the man fell *among thieves*. Take a look at John 10:10.

> *"The thief cometh not, but for to steal, and to*
> *kill, and to destroy: I am come that they might*
> *have life, and that they might have it more abun-*
> *dantly."*- John 10:10

This man seems to have had something taken by the thief. He is just like us, and was stripped of his covering (*or Glory,*) and was left half dead, just as Adam was! *V.31* says that a certain *priest* and *Levite* passed by, (*by chance!*) These groups represented the law. It appears that the law couldn't help the man! They offered no help and were there by chance. (*They were not intentional*) V.33 says that *"a certain Samaritan,"* was journeying and came to where the man was! A journey is (*always*) intentional. This *"Samaritan"* sounds a lot like Jesus! He always intentionally comes to *where we are. Religion says we go to Him!* This man had compassion, just like Jesus. V.34 says that He poured in *oil* and *wine*. It's interesting that biblical *oil* always represents (*anointing*) and wine represents (*the blood.*) You could say that *"Jesus poured in His anointing and His blood to heal us after binding up our spiritual wounds!"* The last part of V. 34 says that *the man* took him to *the* _inn_. This sounds an awful lot like the _church_. Wouldn't our church or _the church body of Christ_ be a metaphorical place of safety until Jesus comes back? V.35 makes a few interesting statements. The man gave the _Host_ of the church, (_God,_) two pence which is _(bronze or copper.)_ I would like to note that biblical bronze means judgment. I find it interesting that the man gave two pence, or _(it cost him something through sacrifice or judgment.)_ In V.35, the man in the Bible said He would come back and pay the remaining wage, after paying (_two pence,_) or two days wages.

> **"But, beloved, be not ignorant of this one thing,**
> **that one day is with the Lord as a thousand years,**
> **and a thousand years as one day."**- 2 Peter 3:8

This story tells the accurate account of our Father in Heaven and how He loved us so deeply that He gave His Son for us!

ABRAHAM AND ISAAC MYSTERY

There is another profound message in scripture mentioned a little later in the Bible. The scripture reveals this very same message of love, which included Abraham and his son Isaac. You will love this parallel. As you begin to read the book of Genesis, Abraham was told by God to go to the mountain and slay his son. It is in this story, _(found in the Old Testament)_ the first use of the English Word **Love** appears. Abraham has a first born son (_Isaac_) and God tells Abraham to take his son, _"His one and only son,"_ to make a sacrifice. _(Hint- John 3:16.)_ God is simply trying to show his **friend** Abraham what He would have to go through. I am not going to elaborate on the story much. I will simply give you the nugget and let you dig for yourself.

> **"And he said, Take now thy son, thine only son**
> **Isaac, whom thou lovest, and get thee into the**
> **land of Moriah; and offer him there for a burnt**
> **offering upon one of the mountains which I will**
> **tell thee of."**- Genesis 22:2

In this story *(Also a spiritual parallel)* Isaac represents Jesus. Abraham represents God." He is offered as a burnt offering. Hmm... it sounds a lot like Jesus going to the cross. Then you hear in V.3 that Abraham took two young men with him. Read this next part.

> ***"And Abraham took the wood of the burnt offering, and laid it upon Isaac his son; and he took the fire in his hand, and a knife; and they went both of them together."*** - Genesis 22:6

That sounds a lot like a picture of another man I've heard of, named Jesus! That would parallel, if God would have taken the cross as a burnt offering from Jesus. We keep reading here.

> V.7 ***"And Isaac spake unto Abraham his father, and said, My father: and he said, Here am I, my son. And he said, Behold the fire and the wood: but where is the lamb for a burnt offering?"***

This is an interesting statement because how would Isaac know that he needed a burnt offering of a lamb, *unless he* had heard of the lamb, prior to this point? I Think God must have revealed this knowledge to Isaac as he grew up. He must have been taught. *Isaac just lays upon the wood and never complains, which sounds like something I've heard somewhere else!*

> ***"He was oppressed, and He was afflicted, yet He opened not his mouth: He is brought as a lamb to the slaughter, and as a sheep before her shearers is dumb, so he openeth not his mouth."*** -
> Isaiah 53:7

This, my friends, is a picture of Jesus! In verse *eight*, something fascinating happens. Abraham says, "God will provide *"Himself"* a lamb. He did *not* say God will provide a lamb. He said *"Himself"*! in V.9, Abraham builds an altar, *(which sounds like a cross,)* because the bible says, *"in order."* Isaac was laid upon it. ***Just*** *like Jesus!* After Abraham is told to slay Isaac in vs.10, something amazing happens in V.13.

> *"And Abraham lifted up his eyes, and looked, and behold behind him a ram caught in a thicket by his horns: and Abraham went and took the ram, and offered him up for a burnt offering in place of his son."*-Genesis 22:13

A Ram in a thicket? Or could this be pointing to Jesus or *"Lamb in the thicket?"* Thicket means *"Thorns."* Rams use their *"head"* which is the most humbling and painful way to be wounded." If you read carefully you will also notice that Abraham says, *"He lifted up his head and saw it behind him?"* How did he see behind him, if He looked up? You can easily see that this is pointing the reader to something much bigger. Based upon the fact that Isaac knew there was supposed to be a sacrificed lamb, this was a picture of Abraham and Isaac acting in faith because God had already promised Abraham that his seed (*offspring*) would out number the stars. This was an act of faith because Abraham knew if he would trust God, then Isaac must have to be saved, and resurrected. He was not using his own understanding. Proverbs *3:4-7*

> *"Trust in the Lord with all thine heart; and lean not unto thine own understanding. In all thy ways acknowledge him, and he shall direct thy paths. Be not wise in thine own eyes: fear the Lord, and depart from evil."*-Proverbs *3:4-7*

Abraham wouldn't have wanted to lose his son after finally being blessed at such an old age. This was Faith! I would like to make another point, as I stated earlier in the book. God added Aleph Tav to anyone who would get into a covenant with Him. You will see in the original Hebrew text, that the moment *"Abram"* listened to God, he received a new name! *"Abraham."*

Chapter 8

TRADITIONS, MYTHS & THE UNDERWORLD

DID CAIN GO TO HELL FOR MURDER? "RELIGION SAYS OF COURSE !"

Yes, It's true! Cain committed murder, but it's possible if God gave him a lifetime to repent, then Cain could have been redeemed. Let's take a look. I'm not trying to convince you that he did go to heaven, but rather allow scripture, not man's opinion to make your decision. I encourage you to check the scripture for yourself. Let me bring a few things to your attention. Cain's son and grandchildren have the names of God, in the Hebrew. He and his wife conceived.

> *"And Cain knew his wife; and she conceived, and bare Enoch: and he builded a city, and called the name of the city, after the name of his son, Enoch. And unto Enoch was born Irad: and Irad begat Mehujael: and Mehujael begat Methusael: and Methusael begat Lamech."*- Genesis 4: 17

Here you'll notice Enoch and *Mehujael and Methusael* have suffixes, which are referring to God. It is odd that God would include these two names with these suffixes and have no purpose whatsoever. I'll leave this one up to you! It turns out that in the book of Jude chapter one, it makes an interesting comment of Cain's first son Enoch.

> *"And Enoch also, the seventh from Adam, prophesied of these, saying, Behold, the Lord cometh with ten thousands of his saints," (Jude is the very first Prophet in the bible!"*- Jude 1:14

Cain's son would be a 3rd generation prophet who would proclaim our Lord Jesus Christ! *Is it possible that Just Like Nicodemus*, we could have a story of redemption? You decide. Don't let religion decide!

WHAT DOES TITHE REALLY MEAN?

Tithing is first mentioned in the garden, in the book of Genesis.

> *"And she again bare his brother Abel. And Abel was a keeper of sheep, but Cain was a tiller of the ground."*- Genesis 4:2

> *"And in process of time it came to pass, that Cain brought of the fruit of the ground an offering unto the Lord."*-Genesis 4:3

It is important to notice two things here:

Cain brought the wrong offering (*"The fruit of the ground"*)(*works*)

1. Cain brought the wrong offering and it wasn't first! (*in the process of time*)

2. Able brought the right offering (His flock) *(blood offering)*

3. Able brought the right offering and it was first *"his Firstlings"or in a hurry*

Let's move on to the book of Malachi. The religious crowd says:"Why do we have to give a church our money? This can easily be used as a reason to deny God what is his so let me take you to the book of Malachi Chapter three.

WHAT IS THE TITHE AND OFFERING? HOW MUCH?

> *"Will a man rob God? Yet ye have robbed me. But ye say, Wherein have we robbed thee? In tithes and offerings. "*- Malachi 3:8

There it is! let's move on to find out a couple of things about this scripture. What does scripture say? V.8 says, *"Will a man rob God? Yet ye have robbed me. But ye say, Wherein have we robbed thee? In tithes and offerings." V.9 "Ye are cursed with a curse: for ye have robbed me, even this whole nation."*

God has made this very clear in scripture. He says you not only rob Me, but you rob the entire nation, who would have been blessed by your obedience! You might ask,*"What church or where do I send it?"* The answer is in V.10. A tithe can be any form of your available gain, or income such as Mary and Joseph giving a turtle dove. Anything of value. God doesn't care if your balloon is big or little, He only cares that we offer based upon its capacity and its potential. He doesn't want a giant balloon with a little air. He would rather have a little balloon with its maximum air. He sees the little balloon first! He doesn't need our money. He is after our *heart*. If we pursue His heart rather than His hand, He will in return, offer what is in His hand!

> *"Bring ye all the tithes into the storehouse, that there may be meat in mine house, and prove me now herewith, saith the Lord of hosts, if I will not open you the windows of heaven, and pour*

you out a blessing, that there shall not be room enough to receive it."- Malachi 3:10

The root word of the tithe comes from the Hebrew, translated into Greek. This word according to H6240 of the concordance means *"Mah-as-raw"* or *"tenth* part." The word storehouse according to H214 of the same, means *"otsar"* or *"treasury, armory or where you receive your treasure.* Let's make this more clear. I would say, *(your church or spiritual feeding source)* would make the most sense. We should sow our first fruits where we are being fed spiritually! Let me mention God's principal parable, and show you how it perfectly explains the most important spiritual truth that is outlined here. *You reap what you sow!*

"Be not deceived; God is not mocked: for whatsoever a man soweth, that shall he also reap."- Galatians 6:7

"And he spake many things unto them in parables, saying, Behold, a sower went forth to sow;"- Matthew 13:3

Luke 8:4-15 will list the parable of the four sowers, which I encourage you to read, but for now I will show the first one mentioned. Normally God's Word (*as I've said before*) will follow the law of first mention. I want to note this first parable.

"Hearken; Behold, there went out a sower to sow:"- Mark 4:3

The rest is up to you the reader!!

P.S. Your tax return is exactly what it says! If you tithed your first tenth of your entire increase, or first fruit, then you've already paid it forward. One hundred percent of that return is yours, because it was taken from you, and wasn't an increase! *Merry Christmas,* your offering is anything above and beyond what is God's already. Example *(buying someone food, doing a good deed, etc)*

IS HADES, HELL?

Not exactly! Religion clouds the truth so it won't offend so many people! Lets begin to look at this religiously taught misconception. To begin with, it depends upon whether or not we read the King James Bible. The majority of our currently used Bibles, such as the *NIV* version, have added the word Hades, typically in place of the word (*Hell*) such as in the King James Bible passage here...

> *"I am he that liveth, and was dead; and behold, I am alive for evermore, Amen; and have the keys of hell and of death."*-Revelation 1:18

If you read this same verse in the NIV version it reads like this...

> *"I am the Living One; I was dead, and now look, I am alive for ever and ever! And I hold the keys of death and hades."*-Revelation 1:18

These two verses are entirely different! Let me show you something. The word *"Sheol"* is the Hebrew word for *"abode of the dead,"* which is called hades, was used in the Old Testament. This is not hell, but where the dead go. At this time, Jesus had not been resurrected yet, hence no opportunity to ascend into heaven to the right hand of the Father. There had to be a place for the believers and non believers of Jesus to go before His ascension. Let me explain further. If we read the book of *Luke 16:19*, you will see a story of a rich man and a man named Lazarus. Lazarus was a man who was sick, poor and hungry. The rich man would not even offer him food or help and both of these men died at the same time.

> *"There was a certain beggar named Lazarus, which was laid at his gate, full or sores."*- Luke 16:19

Where did Jesus go to preach when He died? Later in another verse it says this...

> *"And it came to pass, that the beggar died, and was carried by the angels into Abraham's bosom: the rich man also died, and was buried."*-Luke 16:22

Side note: Notice that the bad man was carried nowhere but the good man, Lazarus was carried off by angels. The Bible states that the rich man was simply *"buried,"* end of the story! No need to give him anymore airtime. God had his focus on the man's obedience. .

> *"And in Hell he lift up his eyes, being in torments, and seeth Abraham afar off, and Lazarus in his bosom."*- Luke 16:23

In this part of the story you will notice that somehow the rich man's perspective was from hell but Lazarus's view was in *Abraham's bosom.*

> *"And beside all this, between us and you there is a great gulf fixed: so that they which would pass from hence to you cannot; neither can they pass to us, that would come from thence."*- Luke 16:26

It is very apparent that there is a clear separation between the two places, which lets the reader know that this place is irreversible and permanent. The rich man is fully aware of his surroundings, and has memories, pains and desires. He asks for his brothers to be spared and wants to warn them of this awful place. *The rich man went directly to his final judgment!* He was aware that he was on the bad side of hades!

Please take note also here that Lazarus has no dialog, just the rich man. I would assume this makes sense considering that if he is not in hell then he wouldn't have had the knowledge of the rich man being present in torment. One man named Dante once said, this place was a place to abandon all hope! The rich man on the other hand has not decided to live the right life and is clearly seen here in torment. At this point his destiny is unchangeable just like hell and he acknowledges that he is in hell. You will also notice that Lazarus was carried off to a place called (*Abraham's bosom,*) which is very interesting. It is widely believed by most Bible scholars that God emptied the good side of Abraham's bosom, (*The faithful people such as Lazarus,*) to Himself!

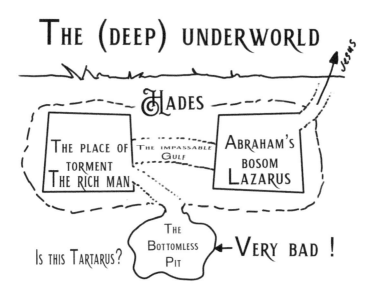

Hades, the abode of the dead

I am taking you to a place that would appear to be a critical part of the Word of God. This is very useful and gives us a clear picture of Hades, which is, *"The abode of the dead,"* *"not hell,"* or in some cases known as *"A holding cell, or a place of temporary stay until Jesus ascends to the right hand of the father."* It is a place where people are held captive until eternal death. Please let me explain. If you read Jesus's conversation with the 2 men on the cross, here.

"And he said unto Jesus, Lord, remember me when thou comest into thy kingdom."-Luke 23:42

"And Jesus said unto him, Verily I say unto thee, Today shalt thou be with me in paradise."-Luke 23:43

In *Luke 23:42,* Jesus mentions His kingdom and He mentions *paradise,* which refers to a garden and not the throne of God. If you study the Greek, you will discover that Jesus was not sent to heaven the day He died, because we know He was buried *three* days and three nights.

Another account of Jesus says…

"Jesus saith unto her, Touch me not; for I am not yet ascended to my Father: but go to my brethren, and say unto them, I ascend unto my Father; and to my God, and your God."-John 20:17

You may also notice in these verses...

"For Christ also hath once suffered for sins, the just for the unjust, that he might bring us to God, being put to death in the flesh, but quickened by the spirit."-1 Peter 3:18

"If I ascend up into heaven, thou art there: if I make my bed in hell, behold, thou art there."-Psalms 139:8

"By which also he went and preached unto the spirits in prison."-1 Peter 3:19

We know that Jesus went somewhere to preach after dying, before ascending to heaven and my only objective here is to bring your attention to these scriptures, as well as the place of paradise and Abraham's bosom. My goal is to guide you, (*the reader,*) to develop a closer relationship with Jesus.

"And the spirit of the Lord shall rest upon him, the spirit of wisdom and understanding, the spirit of counsel and might, the spirit of knowledge and of the fear of the Lord;"-Isaiah 11:2

These seven powerful anointings in our lives will always lead us into truth. This is man-made religion. Let's move on to the Holy Grail of religion. *(If I may use this term loosely)* Lets move to another Lazarus who you will find in the book of John and I think this will take us out with a *big bang*!

It appears that this is a literal story, not a parable. God never used a person by name if his only intent was to tell a parable. *This is another religious belief.* Many people often try to destroy the story of *Luke 16:19.* I would venture to guess that if we believed this story (*of where we would go after living a life without God*) then the painful truth would be revealed! Not having God in our hearts would be too much for some readers to accept. Wow! this just might force the religious crowd to change their lives. *Please read it for yourself.* I am simply saying it seems to clearly imply that Hades *(Hell)* is real. And there is also a place that is not hell, called Hades, which is reserved for the dead, whom Jesus likely ministered to!

LAZARUS COME FORTH!

> *"And when he thus had spoken, he cried with a loud voice, Lazarus, come forth."*-John 11:43

"This oddly rings in my ears another powerful statement!"

> *"And about the ninth hour Jesus cried with a loud voice, saying, Eli, Eli, lama sabachthani? that is to say, My God, my God, why hast thou forsaken me?"*-Matthew 27:46

I think what I am pointing out is that when Jesus cries out with a loud voice, that maybe He is passionate when He speaks this way. Maybe when He is yelling with His entire heart, He is making a *very important* statement. Maybe He is desperately trying to reveal to us a spiritual principle! *"Lazarus, come forth from the grave!"* Maybe He is saying *"Lazarus"* who is bound by *"grave clothes"* or maybe, *"hey Christian"*, who is bound by religion! *"Please shake off your affliction, that's holding you down."* *"Hey Christian, (Lazarus,) you're not dead!"* *"Listen to my voice and walk forward,"* and *"shake off that death"* or **religion,** *that has you dead without following My voice! I am telling you that I love you and if you will just follow My voice, and no one else's, I'll reveal Myself to you as soon as you walk out of the grave! I'm the good Shepherd! Stop listening to men! The religion is literally killing you!*

Religion is what killed Jesus's body to begin with! Jesus spoke these last words on the cross and said, *"Tetelestai"* or "a battle had been won, or a debt had been paid.

> **"When Jesus therefore had received the vinegar, he said, It is finished: and he bowed his head, and gave up the ghost."**- John 19:30

It's almost as if He bowed His head from the death of this world. We should bow our heads in prayer in the same sense, as if to give honor to Jesus and say, *"we are willing to die of this world to be with You in Paradise! We will bow our heads too!"* These words are what compel me to worship differently and to pray differently! We should revere him! The apostle Paul said it best:

> **"For the love of Christ constraineth us; because we thus judge, that if one died at all, then were all dead:"**-2 Corinthians 5:14

This is like saying, "His love compels me so much that I'm con-victed so much that I'll serve Him forever and ever! He died for me and I can't *not* love him!

TABOO: DEATH, MARRIAGE, HOMOSEXUALITY, AND ABORTION

DEATH IS VICTORY, NOT A TRAGEDY

> *"For to me to live is Christ, and to die is gain."*-Phi-lippians 1:21

Religion makes death about loss. We are all affected by death, but the truth is, we are created by God, and only our Creator has the dominion over His creation. God will take back what He created. We are born into sinful flesh. Believe it or not, Jesus was born into sinful flesh as well, but *(never sinned Himself)*

> *"For he hath made him to be sin for us, who knew no sin; that we might be made the righteousness of God in Him."*- *2 Corinthians 5:21*

> *"For what the law could not do, in that it was weak through the flesh, God sending His own Son in the likeness of sinful flesh, and for sin, condemned sin in the flesh:"*- Romans 8:3

Because of our sinful flesh, we are under the judgment of death...

> *"Wherefore, as by one man sin entered into the world, and death by sin; and so death passed upon all men, for that all have sinned:"*-Romans 5:12

> *"For the wages of sin is death; but the gift of God is eternal life through Jesus Christ our Lord."*-Romans 6:23

No one took the life of Jesus, He gave it! Our sin compelled Him to sacrifice Himself!

We are born to glorify God! Jesus's death was not a tragedy, it was a victory! Likewise, our death is not a tragedy! If we are following Jesus, then we shouldn't spend our time investing in the knowledge of the dead. We should celebrate our loved ones while they are alive. God doesn't need our religious rituals. When we lose the body of a loved one to the dust, they vacate earth, and return home. We are truly only dead when we return to the ground where we came from. We're the ones that suffer.

> *"Therefore we are always confident, knowing that, whilst we are at home in the body, we are absent from the Lord:"*-2 Corinthians 5:6

> *"We are confident, I say, and willing rather to be absent from the body, and to be present with the Lord."*-2 Corinthians 5:8

God knitted us in our mother's womb. God originally made us in His image before sin entered in. He wrapped us in glory, before we sinned. We adopted a flesh body, containing a spirit, that possesses a soul.

> *"Before I formed thee in the belly I knew thee; and before thou camest forth out of the womb I sanctified thee, and I ordained thee a prophet unto the nations."*-*Jeremiah 1:5*

> *"But I would not have you to be ignorant, brethren, concerning them which are asleep, that ye sorrow not, even as others which have no hope."*-1 Thessalonians 4:13

> *"Yea, though I walk through the valley of the shadow of death, I will fear no evil: for thou art*

with me; thy rod and thy staff they comfort me."-
Psalms 23: 4

F.E.A.R = (__F__alse-__E__vidence-__A__ppearing-__R__eal) religion says, "honor the dead," God says to honor the living!"

This may not be a popular statement, but when our loved ones die and are buried, they leave their bodies. *A perfect example is Luke 16:23.* This is the same as moving out of a *house* and relocating! We leave our body at the moment of death! You may have heard, *"home is where the heart is." A house is a house, but a home is what dwells inside of it!*

It's interesting to note that anything put into the earth becomes part of it. Our flesh came from the earth and will return to it. You have heard of cremation (*similar to creation*) and it's total destruction of DNA by fire. This is the point when the human flesh no longer has any identification whatsoever. It was only after God breathed life into our bodies, that He gave us living DNA. When we die, it is entirely removed after returning to the sinful earth. This will make you think!

I would like to mention one interesting side note about our flesh. There is an interesting cell adhesion protein molecule called *Laminin.* that just so happens to hold our entire body together. This is essentially a cell with (*mechanical scaffolding*) properties that are quite literally the glue that holds our entire bodies together. I find it interesting that the protein cell that holds our entire physical bodies together happens to look exactly the same as the cross! *This will make you think!*

Laminin

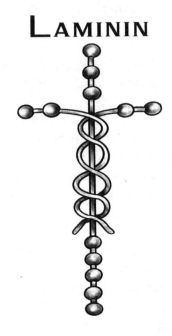

Laminin, or glue that holds us together

MARRIAGE

Many people ask me if we will be married in heaven. The answer is YES, to God, NOT each other! The Bible gives a clear understanding of this subject.

WE ARE NOT ANGELS OR GIVEN IN MARRIAGE, IN HEAVEN!

> **"For in the resurrection they <u>neither marry</u>, nor are given in marriage, but are <u>as</u> the angels of God in heaven."**- Matthew *23:30*

We are <u>similar</u>, just like we become *similar* to Jesus, in heaven, but we ***don't* <u>become</u>** Him!

"Husbands, love your wives, even as Christ also loved the church, and gave himself for it;."-
Ephesians 5:25

God calls Jesus, the *groom*, and calls *the church*, his bride. *This refers to you and me.* It is very clear to me that marriage was established, in the garden, as a way for God to paint a beautiful picture of our relationship in heaven with Himself. The word marriage literally means, *husband* and *wife*. I'll go into this further in the next section.

"Yet ye say, Wherefore? Because the Lord hath been witness between thee and the wife of thy youth, against whom thou hast dealt treacherously: yet is she thy companion, and the wife of thy covenant."-Malachi 2:14

God gave us this amazing Covenant on earth to express His loving relationship with us. This is why He paints such a glorious picture of Eden. (*Pleasure*) We cannot begin to grasp the marriage supper of Revelation, so He lovingly gives us an earthy picture of it! We will no longer need (*our version*) of marriage, once we are with the Father.

There is a trending chauvinist belief system in religion, that says man is to rule over his wife, in some demeaning and controlling way. The Bible says something different, when kept in context. The Bible doesn't say that a rib was taken out of Adam's foot and given to Eve (*to be stepped on*) but rather his side. The rib was taken from his side to share with her! I want you to look at this scripture with me carefully.

"But I would have you know, that the head of every man is Christ; and the head of the woman is the man; and the head of Christ is God." God has laid out his plan for the church and its structure. This is further expressed in the book of Ephesians

5:22 " *Wives, submit yourselves unto your own husbands, as unto the Lord.* "- 1 Corinthians 11:3

God must have an assigned order. There must be an order in God's kingdom, just as any business partnership. Can you imagine working for a company where there are two spokesmen and you have no idea whose word is final? This is not some religious order put in place to condemn one or elevate the other. This is God's plan and abiding in it, means abiding in Him. The woman is to submit to God's authority, by submitting to her husband and the same goes for the husband to his wife. They are to submit to one another according to God's plan. This is not to identify our own fleshly, prideful needs. Man and woman should desire to follow God's structure to glorify Him! This leads to the man and the woman actually, *desiring* one another even more! They can begin to purposely serve the other, and as a response of the other person's love for God. Marriage is like chess. The king isn't dangerous in any way, but He is the focus of leadership. On the other hand, the queen is mighty, and has complete control of the board. The enemy will always take out the queen first! She is a threat. Remember the garden? Adam was alone with the serpent. Satan was the only beast who was intelligent and able to communicate. One meaning of the word satan, in the Hebrew Bible is; *false accuser, seducer, beautiful or even shiny.* Is't it interesting that when satan saw this *(likely beautiful)* woman, that he immediately went after *(the queen.)* Satan knew that if he deceived her, the man would save her, and take the sin upon himself. *(Jesus did the same for us!) God gave us women to love, and cherish, because He loves us so much. There is a reason why weddings always honor the women, by asking everyone to stand. God did the same, by blessing Eve with the seed of life. We should open the door for women, in reverence of God's picture of love!* Marriage is a picture of heaven!

HOMOSEXUALITY

I know that this subject tends to be *subjective.* I could easily mention several scriptures relating to this subject, but I wanted to take a different approach concerning homosexuality. I am not writing about my thoughts and opinions or view of who is sinning and who is not. I only have a few things to mention. Creation was designed with a *man and a woman.* Creation can not advance in any other form. God loves creation so much that He created over *seven billion* people to express His love, by forming a man and a woman. It would appear to me that God would bless the union *in covenant*, to the advancement of that fact. My opinion has nothing to do with what I want to show you.

I was approached by a *"Legally bound female couple."* One of them asked me, *"why would God keep me from intimately being with my spouse, if we love each other?"* I knew that the moment I took a stance, one way or another, that it was a *"lose-lose" answer, in her eyes.* If I would have said *"It's wrong,"* she would say, *"You can't judge,"* and if I were to say it's alright, then I would be accused of being *"anti-God,"* by the Christian community. There is only one correct answer *in my opinion.* I could easily take the side of what I believe is truth, and tell her why the Bible says it's wrong, in which she would have just felt condemnation, or I could take the approach of love, and give her an example of how God sees it. *Here's what I told her...*

"What if I fell in love with my neighbor's wife? She is so beautiful, and I love her!"

If God says something is not good, then we should obey Him. Just because we desire something or someone, doesn't mean that we make the rules. My goal is not to tell you what is right or wrong, *(that is the Holy Spirit's job)* but rather lead you to the truth of God's Word, and leave the religion out of it. The closer a person gets to truth, the more willing they are to receive that deeper thing of God.

"He that is faithful in that which is least is faithful also in much: and he that is unjust in the least is unjust also in much."-
Luke 16:10

If someone shuts down due to the feeling of judgment, they will never be willing to receive. The answer is *conviction*, not *condemnation*. Conviction can be defined as *the moment that we decide to take sides with God against our own sin!* We have to lead with sensitivity, but lead with truth! When Peter apologizes to Jesus for betraying Him, Jesus only asks Peter if he loved Him. Jesus never said *"Peter, you messed up, but do you love me?"* Jesus only cares that we love Him.

ABORTION

Let me bring up another question that I hear all of the time. *It's my body."* I'm sure many of you have heard this, so let's take a different look at it. *If I handed you my phone, would it be your phone? Of course not!* You would be the *carrier who was chosen to be the vessel, in which it would be sustained until I wanted it back.* Human beings are very much the same way. Women have genetic properties that make them perfect avatars to house God's most precious creations, with men being used in perfect conjunction. We don't own them, just as a mother doesn't own her *thirty eight* year old son. They would feel (*Storge*) love and connection to them, but still would not be their Creator.

There are a few other things that I have heard. Here is an example. *"What if my baby wasn't planned, like rape, incest, or it if it was against my will?"* or *"What if a doctor tells me that the baby may have birth defects?"* These are all extremely valid, and painful decisions to face, I'm sure. I'm not God and I've never been a woman, so my answer would be legalistic or religious. I do however have some scriptures to show you that would allow the Holy Spirit to speak to you in truth. Here are *three* facts found in the Word of God. Please read these first until the very end. I think a very powerful point that can be revealed!

Life is in the blood.

> **"For the life of the flesh is in the blood: and I have given it to you upon the altar to make an atonement for your souls: for it is the blood that maketh an atonement for the soul."**-Leviticus 17:11

It turns out that if you study the developmental life cycle of a child, you'll realize that the very first moment of life in the womb is *one single drop of blood!*

1.   *God hates murder, (innocent blood shed.)*

2.   **"These six things doth the Lord hate: yea, seven are an abomination unto him:" V.17 "A proud look, a lying tongue, and hands that shed innocent blood,"**-Proverbs 6:16-17 V.16

I want to point out that murder by definition is *(To put an end to,) (according the the Meriam Dictionary.)* It can also mean to *(switch off or destroy.) Satan is the destroyer,* according to John 10:10. This is obviously not one of God's attributes.

3.   *John is (alive) in the womb!*

4.   **"And it came to pass, that when Elisabeth heard the salutation of Mary, the babe leaped in her womb; and Elisabeth was filled with the Holy Ghost:"**- Luke 1:41

Here is the clear revelation that the Holy Spirit has given me. God is against murder by taking someone's life which He created. (*Murder is destruction, invented by satan,*) and God clearly gave John the Baptist life inside his mother's womb. This is in clear opposition to death, which only leads me to one conclusion. No matter what our pains are in life, whether it is a woman giving birth, or a man in dire pain, we are **not** God! That's how Adam and Eve failed in the garden to begin with! We cannot determine the beginning stages of life! Whether inside or outside of the womb, as a baby can't speak at the age of one, drive at the age of *five,* or run a business at the age of ten. The truth is at any stage of our life cycle, we are alive and the only true line that can be drawn in the sand, is with God Himself. I think by now we have established His heart.

*Here's my answer to the question of abortion, based upon all of these facts. If you decide to take the life of a human being (at any developmental stage,) then I suppose you have to decide if **your pain** is more important than **Gods!** If we are God, then we decide!*

Chapter 9

PSYCHOLOGY- LOVE AND ANOINTING OILS

Let's address the subject of mental illness. I think there are so many people in the world today who suffer from a variety of different physiological and mental hurdles. I think so often people tend to be overlooked or somehow put in a box that says they should be embarrassed or separated from society. During the time the Bible was written, a person would have been outcast for reasons such as mental illnesses or (*non-norm*) deformities or even pregnancy. Since the beginning of time we have outcast people and made them feel as though their ailments were somehow worse than another. I am passionate about bringing to light some conditions or personality traits that I believe religion has cast a shadow over. Medical professionals & psychologists have convinced most of these people to feel as though they have a condition that sets them apart from society, leaving them to feel ashamed and inferior to the rest of the world. *This is simply not true*! These people are just as valuable and worthy as any other person walking the face of the earth. I want this section of my book to be received as an eye opening look at the mental diversity around the world. Maybe with a little understanding we can observe their need and collectively offer them more useful input that will, in return, help them cope with the world we live in.

SYNDROMES OR DISORDERS

VICTIM MENTALITY "SYNDROME"

Have you ever been told growing up that you had a problem? Have you ever been led to believe something about yourself and you heard it so long that you began to believe it?

We have all been the victim of self doubt or felt defeated. God made us the victor, not *the victim!*

In the book of Genesis we see Adam and Eve blaming someone else. It's *"the blame game,"* which leads to the victim mentality. Adam blames the woman for his failure, and Eve blames the serpent. In the book of Genesis, Adam blames the woman for his mistake.

> *"And the man said, The woman whom thou gavest to be with me, she gave me of the tree, and I did eat."*-Genesis 3:12

From this point we see the woman blame the serpent…

> *"And the Lord God said unto the woman, What is this that thou hast done? And the woman said, The serpent beguiled me, and I did eat."*-Genesis 3:13

My only reason for making this point is to show that we have the ability to be the victor, rather than the victim, who takes the side of pity. I think many of us blame our failures on our parents, or ex's, or the government. We have the power of the Holy Spirit. We should hold ourselves accountable. The Bible mentions a very real truth about (*playing the victim.*) We have the ability to save ourselves, in most cases. God gives us the choice to lay in bed or to get up and take over the world! We shouldn't look at someone else's life and judge our own based upon theirs. We should make the most of our own life, with the help of Jesus. All things are possible! There was a man who was at the Pool of Bethesda who had an infirmity for *thirty eight* years. Jesus came to him and said, *"wilt thou be made whole?"* Jesus asks the man if he could help himself. Jesus doesn't ask a question because He doesn't know the answer, He asks because He wants to know if we do! Jesus clearly wanted the man to know that if he would just stand up and *stop* feeling victimized, and walk, then he could save himself.

Don't let a psychologist, friends, or even the news, tell you that you are **lost**, broken, unfixable or worthless. Most of your conditions can be fixed with faith in God, and prayer. If anyone tells you that you are *lost*, you should rejoice because that means you are loved by someone. If you were just *misplaced*, then that would mean you were just somewhere and knowone cares! When we lose something, we have a purpose for it before it is lost and we search like crazy. When we *misplace* something, it means that it never had a place or an origin! Thank God that when we are lost, Jesus comes to find us!

PSYCHOLOGY-THE "SCIENTIFIC?" STUDY OF THE MIND & BEHAVIOR

I've made a small list of people mentioned in the Bible who were all going through mental battles, (*or spiritual,*) you decide. Most of them were affected by one spiritual thing or another. I'll put these examples in a box to draw a parallel of how our physiological, "experts" would tend to label them. I am not saying that the people I mention had these conditions. I am saying if we put them in a giant pool of people with similar issues, then psychologists might draw these conclusions.

Nebuchadnezzar- *Schizophrenia?* —-He acted like an animal!

Job- *Clinical Depression?* —-After losing everything!

Paul- _Post Traumatic stress (PTSD)_ after all the Christian murders he committed? _Jesus_—-In the Garden of Gethsemane. Classic anxiety (_what he was about to do_). Also at the tomb of Lazarus, weeping in _depression_ where he was resuscitated and became _bipolar, right?_

Psalms—-The psalmist himself expresses all forms of these illnesses, _right?_

Does this mean that every single person in the Bible has mental illnesses? All of them were subjected to mental anguish or some extraordinary circumstances. Maybe the're just human beings who are different from one another! I think the answer is, _"you decide."_

There are bi-polar disorders; _(depression, social anxiety disorders or general sadness disorders.)_

We have made mental illness the new normal trend. _ADD (Attention Deficit Disorder)_ or _ADHD (Attentions Deficit Hyper Disorder.)_ These can even become our identity. A Lot of times we will reveal our condition before our own name. For example, _"Hello, I have a chemical imbalance and my name is John."_ There is also a _"syndrome"_ called post _traumatic stress disorder,_ and you can never get away from the famous, _"Chemical Imbalance." We have been psychologized._ So often we avoid our pastor, but talk to a psychologist (_who by the way, is simply a person who went to college for four years and in most cases, feel they have all the answers.)_ This is not to take away from the career field of psychology, but is often the only go to source, rather than spiritual guidance. Note: _Most college students take psychology._

All of these people have definitive and legitimate mental situations that differ in symptoms. I am not saying mental illnesses are not real. Quite the opposite, but my point is that religion plays such a large role in misleading people into believing they have what I call, the (_human condition._) That is to say that God made us all completely different, like individual snowflakes. Science so often tries to take a religious or legalistic approach at labeling these people and have convinced the general public that they are different from the next person, (*no matter how extreme.*) **Science has nothing to do with it!** I know you are reading this and you are thinking that some people are extremely affected by mental illness and need medication. This may very well be the case!

The point I'm making is that society has tried to make the psychiatrist a *g*od, rather than **God**, being God! There is an interesting thing called (*over diagnosis.*) I could easily give you a long list of (*so called mental disorders,*) and it is very likely that most of you reading this have either been diagnosed with or could say, yes, it affects me! Words like *syndrome* or *condition* are used frequently because there is no diagnosis. The reason psychologists prescribe new medications is because the first one didn't work, so the patient is drugged and they move on to the next prescription! I am not minimizing anyone that we may know, or their diagnosis or human condition, but I am rather asking you to read further and at least observe what I'm about to say before coming to any conclusions.

A determination of a diagnosis is made by a group of people in psychological communities, who sit around a table with a group of different symptoms affecting their patients, and together, they establish a name for each "*so called*" condition, or (*chemical imbalance.*) You may ask why this happens. This is because once a diagnosis has been established, then major *insurance companies will pay for it!* Unfortunately, there has never been a test for it, ***ever***! God made us completely correct and He didn't make a mistake in doing so. Satan used Eve to usher in sin and our world has been fractured ever since! We were covered in Glory from the Garden of Eden. It was perfect, there wasn't any sin, disease or mental illness. Mental illness is not like blood pressure, which can be scientifically tested and adjusted. I hope anyone reading this will understand that I respect and fully understand that many people suffer from irregular mental conditions and my heart goes out to them. In conclusion, maybe we should consult spiritual counsel first, (*considering that God created our minds*) and spend less time taking the avenue of trusting man!

CAN WE USE ANOINTING OILS TO HEAL?

"And they cast out many devils, and anointed with oil many that were sick, and healed them."- Mark 6:13

It is important to note that these people were going out to identify certain individuals. Jesus sent them out to do a specific job for Him. God was using this as a healing. This was not for the people themselves. We have made this a religious practice that we use for ourselves. Another case where anointing oils were used was in the book of *Mark 14:3-9*

"And being in Bethany in the house of Simon the leper, as he sat at meat, there came a woman having an alabaster box of ointment of spike-nard very precious; and she brake the box, and poured it on his head. And there were some that had indignation within themselves, and said, Why was this waste of the ointment made? For it might have been sold for more than three hundred pence, and have been given to the poor. And they murmured against her. And Jesus said, Let her alone; why trouble ye her? she hath wrought a good work on me. For ye have the poor with you always, and whensoever ye will ye may do them good: but me ye have not always. She hath done what she could: she is come aforehand to anoint my body to the burying. Verily I say unto you, Wheresoever this gospel shall be preached throughout the whole world, this also that she hath done shall be spoken of for a memorial of her."- Mark 14:3-9

This woman offers something very valuable to use on Jesus. Again this is an anointing of Jesus, not meant for anyone else. There are so many different places in scripture that anointing oils are offered to God, but never in a religious practice offered to anyone else! God doesn't need our religious acts!

Just like in the tabernacle, the altar of incense was only to be offered to God and it was said to be a sweet smell to Him. There is a New Testament verse that I want to point out. I'm sure there are many people who are set on defending the use of anointing oils. They will say, *"This is not the law age, but an age of grace."*

> *"And thou shalt speak unto the children of Israel, saying, This shall be an holy anointing oil unto me throughout your generations. Upon man's flesh shall it not be poured, neither shall ye make any other like it, after the composition of it: it is holy, and it shall be holy unto you. Whosoever compoundeth any like it, or whosoever putteth any of it upon a stranger, shall even be cut off from his people. And the Lord said unto Moses, Take unto thee sweet spices, stacte, and onycha, and galbanum; these sweet spices with pure frankincense: of each shall there be a like weight: And thou shalt make it a perfume, a confection after the art of the apothecary, tempered together, pure and holy: And thou shalt beat some of it very small, and put of it before the testimony in the tabernacle of the congregation, where I will meet with thee: it shall be unto you most holy ."*-Exodus 30:31-36

> *"Is any sick among you? let him call for the elders of the church; and let them pray over him, anointing him with oil in the name of the Lord:"*-James 5:14

Of course in this instance, a religious person would say *"there was a man being anointed with oil, in the New Testament, so isn't that considered anointing oil?"* Some people would use this argument because if oil is being used in the Old Testament, they would ask why oil is being used after Jesus is alive, if oil was only meant for God? This scripture is referencing *(anointing or to rub off.)* The word *sick* here is being used for a *physical* ailment. The elders are told (*according to the Hebrew concordance*) to *rub off* oil *in the medical sense,* to heal a *physical* sickness. The elders were supposed to apply healing oil, and pray with him. If you reference

the story of Jonah and the whale, the Bible says Jonah was *afflicted*.

> *"And said, I cried by reason of mine affliction unto the Lord, and he heard me; out of the belly of hell cried I, and thou heardest my voice."*-Jonah 2:2

Lazarus, on the other hand was *"sick"* and Jesus said this sickness was not unto death"

> *When Jesus heard that, he said, This sickness is not unto death, but for the glory of God, that the Son of God might be glorified thereby."*-John 11:4

Here's the point that I would like to make. There are clear principles all throughout the Bible that consistently point to a couple of facts. First of all, it is clear that a (***sickness***) is of the *flesh* and (***affliction***) references a *spiritual* ailment or parallel. In closing, this scripture in James is saying if someone is sick, they need medicating oil, or possibly medication.

Chapter 10

LOVE & THE GARDEN DECEPTION

WHAT IS LOVE? את

I hope to make a very important statement in this section of my book. Love is portrayed so religiously and skewed and this has led to so many broken relationships. Love is so widely misunderstood. So many times I've talked to young couples married and unmarried. We have these in-depth talks about the meaning of love and making love as well as what love really means. My intent is to biblically define love at its root and to dismantle man's religious version of it. This is God's love.

Love is defined using the word *"Charity"* in the King James Bible.

> *"Charity suffereth long, and is kind; charity envieth not; charity vaunteth not itself, is not puffed up, Doth not behave itself unseemly, seeketh not her own, is not easily provoked, thinketh no evil; Rejoiceth not in iniquity, but rejoiceth in the truth; Beareth all things, believeth all things, hopeth all things, endureth all*

things. Charity never faileth: but whether there be prophecies, they shall fail; whether there be tongues, they shall cease; whether there be knowledge, it shall vanish away.- 1 Corinthians 13:4-8

God gives us a comprehensive list of how love is defined. We tend to try to figure out love on our own and God makes it so simple! Religion says love is an emotion. *Not true!*

GODS DEFINITION OF LOVE

Charity suffers long	*(Love is patient)*
Charity is kind	*(Love is warm hearted)*
Charity is envieth not	*(Love is not jealous)*
Charity vaunteth not itself	*(Love is not boastful)*
Charity is not puffed up	*(Love is not too proud)*
Charity doth not behave itself unseemingly	*(Love is not unbecoming)*
Charity seeketh not her own	*(Love is not selfish)*
Charity is not easily provoked	*(Love is not easily provoked)*
Charity thinketh no evil	*(Love is without evil thoughts)*
Charity rejoices not in iniquity	*(Love is not happy with injustice)*
Charity rejoices in the truth	*(Love is happy with the truth)*
Charity beareth all things	*(Love endures all things)*
Charity believeth all things	*(Love has faith in all things)*
Charity hopeth all things	*(Love expects all things)*
Charity endureth all things	*(Loves bears all things)*
Charity never faileth	*(Love never falls away)*

Now For the truth…

"For we have not followed cunningly devised fables, when we made known unto you the power and coming of our Lord Jesus Christ, but were eyewitnesses of his majesty."- 2 Peter 1:16

This is a product of the gatekeeper! The gatekeepers are the people who control the flow of information. This story among so many others have helped to influence and massively flood the minds of God's children. Satan will always use *fear* to control you. If you are in bondage to a myth or a religion then it becomes the gatekeeper (<u>god</u>) of your soul. Satan wants you to fear everything, but the Bible says *perfect love casts out fear!* You cannot love and fear at the same time. If fear is present then love takes a back seat!

> ***"There is no fear in love; but perfect love casteth out fear: because fear hath torment. He that feareth is not made perfect in love."*** - 1 John 4:18

This is the reason that you would run out in the street to save your child from being hit by an oncoming car. You just react with love because fear has no power! When we fear, we have no room to love. *Check this out*!

> ***"Therefore take no thought, saying, What shall we eat? or, What shall we drink? or, Wherewithal shall we be clothed? (For after all these things do the Gentiles seek:) for your heavenly Father knoweth that ye have need of all these things. But seek ye first the kingdom of God, and his righteousness; and all these things shall be added unto you. Take therefore no thought for the morrow: for the morrow shall take thought for the things of itself. Sufficient unto the day is the evil thereof."*** - Matthew 6:31-34

> ***"No man can serve two masters: for either he will hate the one, and love the other; or else he will hold to the one, and despise the other. Ye cannot serve God and mammon."*** - Matthew 6:24

Mammon is rooted from the word *Hammon*. This is the love of <u>more</u>, as if trusting God and loving, instead of fearing. We cannot

not serve fear if we are serving God. *Love is the same way.* If we are afraid, we are not able to fully love. Let God be our constant and disregard man made religious tales. Most people refer to love as the emotion where two hearts meet. *"they are my soulmate"* or *"our hearts are one"* or *"cupid struck."* All of these statements are biblically inaccurate. Love is not some personal form of satisfaction that just happens. The God of the Bible defines love as a decision upon obedience to His word. There are *four* different main forms of love that I would like to mention:

(Eros Love)- This love is typical of how most relationships start. This love is always about self. This is a love that is self satisfying. It is how someone makes **me** feel. It is a love that makes us feel all warm and fuzzy inside. It is *"erotic love."*

> **"Flee fornication. Every sin that a man doeth is without the body; but he that committeth fornication sinneth against his own body."**-1 Corinthians 6:18

(Phileo Love)-The name adopted from Philadelphia. The city of brotherly love. This is true friendship. It is a gradual development and appreciated friendship. *"Hey man, I love you."* Eros relationships between a man and a woman can slowly develop into this Phileo love. Both kinds of love can develop over time. An example can be the relationship between Jonathan and David in the Bible.

> **"Then Jonathan and David made a covenant, because he loved him as his own soul."**- 1 Samuel 18:3

This scripture is widely misunderstood by the religious crowd. This is a simple example of how a man is loving another man the way God loves. This is so often cynically converted to some sort of perverted meaning.

Here is an example of a conversation between the apostle Peter and Jesus *John 21:15* **"So when they had dined,"** Jesus said to Simon Peter, **"Simon, son of Jonas, lovest thou me more than these?" "He saith unto him, Yea, Lord; thou knowest that I love thee. He saith unto him, feed my lambs."** This was an example of Jesus asking Peter if he loved Him. When Peter responded, he said, *"Yes Jesus, you know I (Phileo)* love you, in the same way a complacent marriage can become, *"Hey baby you know I love you,"* but he rather doesn't really portray authenticity. Jesus on the other hand, is asking a different question than Peter realized. Jesus is asking if Peter *"Agape"* loved him, which I will explain in a moment. They were having a conversation about two different things and Peter doesn't truly understand actual love. I believe that Jesus wanted to know if Peter loved him unconditionally and not because of any circumstance.

(Storge Love)- This love comes from the <u>Noun</u> Greek word, *"Philostorgos"* is the only love that comes out of natural selection or less by choice and more by circumstance. Storge love is how a Mother loves her newborn baby. The baby is born and the mother is immediately completely bonded to her baby. She is led by relationship and not necessarily by decision. This is a natural bond. An example would be *"Mary, Martha and Lazarus"* who were all related.

(Agape Love)- This love is never about self! It is entirely centered around the other person and their needs. It's never fed by one's own self satisfaction. It is when a man or woman through any circumstance stands by their spouse and holds their hair up, or feeds them when they are sick. It's the kind of love that doesn't see itself. Agape love is mentioned in *Corinthians 13:4. "It is patient and kind, etc."* This is what Jesus meant when He was asking Peter if he loved Him. Jesus was referring to Agape love or *(God's Love)*

Finally, Agape love is quite simply *"obedience."* This love involves loving, even when it's not convenient. This love is when someone does you wrong and you love them anyway, because God's word says to just love.

> *"But I say unto you which hear, Love your enemies, do good to them which hate you,"*- Luke 6:27

> *"But I say unto you which hear, Love your enemies, do good to them which hate you,"*- Matthew 5:44

The best example of Agape love would be the scripture where Jesus is being crucified on the cross and they were beating him, mocking him and spitting in his face, rather than Jesus defending Himself, He opened not His mouth.

> *"He was oppressed, and he was afflicted, yet he opened not his mouth: he is brought as a lamb to the slaughter, and as a sheep before her shearers is dumb, so he openeth not his mouth."*- Isaiah 53:7

Jesus makes one of the most bold and obvious statements of love and says:

> *"Then said Jesus, Father, forgive them; for they know not what they do. And they parted his raiment, and cast lots."*-Luke 23:34

> *"Beloved, let us love one another: for love is of God; and every one that loveth is born of God, and knoweth God."*- 1 John 4:7

> *"There is no fear in love; but perfect love casteth out fear: because fear hath torment. He that feareth is not made perfect in love."*- 1 John 4:17

If you are afraid, it cannot be love. If your little baby runs out into the street, you wouldn't stand there and decide on whether or not you would run in the street to save her. Agape love will say, *"I don't care."* You would save her! Love is a choice folks, not an emotion. Oh by the way, I mentioned *"making love"* and this one is simple. If a couple is in a marriage (*which is a covenant*) God should be the center of their marriage, because marriage is a Word designed by God. God uses human marriage so that we understand the relationship between Christ and His church.

> *"Husbands, love your wives, even as Christ also loved the church, and gave himself for it;"*- Ephesians 5:25

When two people are in a Godly relationship, their intimacy should be an appreciation for God's gift of *"Love making."* He offered this to us as a gift that He Himself would be the center of that Love. Making love is (*a man, and a woman and God*)!

DECEPTION, OR LOVE IN THE GARDEN ?

The Garden provided a very important message that must be understood. This message paints a clear picture of our past, present and future that ushered in a love story. God tells us everything we need to know from the very foundation of time. The Garden of Eden meant garden of *"Pleasure."* Yes, I know that religion has *again* twisted an originally beautiful word into a carnal *erotic* misunderstanding. Originally the garden was without sin and no death had been present. Adam and Eve had no knowledge of evil before partaking of the only tree that God said, *"do not touch."* In Genesis *3,* God is dealing with this bad decision and confronts Adam, Eve and the Serpent.

> *"And I will put <u>enmity</u> between thee and the woman, and between thy seed and her seed; it shall bruise thy head, and thou shalt bruise his heel."*- Genesis 3:15

1st MENTION OF THE GOSPEL (*GOOD NEWS*) & *SATAN IS JUDGED!*

Enmity means *hatred*. God didn't create hatred but He would place it between satan and Eve. Satan means *shiny, fiery, bright and beautiful*. Eve means *Mother of all life* or you and Me! This verse is the very first mention of the Gospel, when God said that her seed (*who likely is a reference to Jesus*) will bruise or *(crush)* the head of the serpent's seed (*which is a mortal blow.*) I believe that this happens at the cross. Her seed will only be crushed at the heel (*which is not eternal*) and is just a flesh wound or (*physical death.*) One is flesh and the other is spiritual death! The biggest religious myth about Adam and Eve is how satan ushers in sin, but actually God is showing us the first picture of a love story. <u>God starts His story with love!</u> Just take a look at this...

1 Timothy, Reveals that *Adam was not deceived!*

ADAM WAS NOT DECEIVED!

> *"And Adam was not deceived, but the woman being deceived was in the transgression"*- 1 Timothy 2:14

This story showed us that God loves us. Let me explain. The word Adam means *"Mankind"* or *man. Jesus Christ* was the *Son of God* because He came directly from God. Adam is the first form of *A Son of God* who was originally without sin for the same reason. Jesus would take on the sin of man, and His *(Church,) (Eve.)* Read these verses, *1 Corinthians 15:45-47*

> *V.45 "And so it is written, The first man Adam was made a living soul; the last Adam was made a quickening spirit."*

V.47 "The first man is of the earth, earthy; the second man is the Lord from heaven."-1 Corinthians 15:45-47

"And Adam called his wife's name Eve; because she was the mother of all living"- Genesis 3:20

"The next day John seeth Jesus coming unto him, and saith, Behold the Lamb of God, which taketh away the sin of the world."- John 1:29

His church would represent His bride. That's us!

"Husbands, love your wives, even as Christ also loved the church, and gave himself for it;"- Ephesians 5:25

Take a look at this for a better understanding...

Adam (1st Son of God) Eve (Bride) (Mother of all Life) Genesis 3:20

Jesus (Last Son of God) The Church (Bride)(Us)

Let me break this all down for you. Eve was deceived. Adam was not. Eve would bear the weight of sin but Adam would voluntarily partake so Eve would not bear it alone. Jesus did the very same thing and knowingly would go to the cross with no delay because He loved you and me, just as the first Son of God loved Eve (*His bride.*) Adam would take on sin just as Jesus would at the cross. *This was a love story my friends!* This was a spiritual parallel that would depict to the reader what would follow. The deeper meaning was meant for the reader who will delve deeper into the underlying message.

THE FIRST FRUIT WAS NOT AN APPLE "RELIGION" (*FIG TREE*)

There are so many scriptures in the Bible that are misunderstood in church today. This one might be the most clear and yet most misunderstood sections in Genesis! There is a huge rumor that Eve ate an apple from the Tree of Life. This is *completely false*! We will start with Genesis. Here is the scripture.

> *"And the Lord God planted a garden eastward in Eden; and there he put the man whom he had formed."*- Genesis 2:8

God said eat from the Tree of Life and not the Tree of the knowledge of good and evil.

> *"And the Lord God commanded the man, saying, Of every tree of the garden thou mayest freely eat:"*-Genesis 2:16,17

He follows up with...

> V.17 *"But of the tree of the knowledge of good and evil, thou shalt not eat of it: for in the day that thou eatest thereof thou shalt surely die."*

We keep reading later, in the book of *Genesis,* that the serpent tempts Eve and she is weak and partakes of the fruit.

> *"And when the woman saw that the tree was good for food, and that it was pleasant to the eyes, and a tree to be desired to make one wise, she took of the fruit thereof, and did eat, and gave also unto her husband with her; and he did eat."*- Genesis 3:6

Now we will move on with the truth of this story. Adam and Eve were covered in glory from the beginning before sin came about. There was no death, no pain and no time. The clock started ticking the day sin entered in!

"For thou hast made him a little lower than the angels, and hast crowned him with glory and honour."- Psalms 8:5

THE FIG TREE

We have to look at a few things,so let's look at the Tree of the Knowledge of good and evil and t*he Fig Tree.* It is historical that the fig tree covers up its own fruit and a person wouldn't even know if it bears fruit or not. That seems a lot like the Fig tree that Adam and Eve used to *cover their sin!* The history within history dictates that it kept its leaves year round. Jesus goes to a fig tree *four* days before going to the cross, to see if it has any fruit.

> *"And seeing a fig tree afar off having leaves, he came, if haply he might find any thing thereon: and when he came to it, he found nothing but leaves; for the time of figs was not yet."*- Mark 11:13

Jesus speaks to the tree and says, no man should eat of it. *He even hears Peter say this in Mark.*

> *"And in the morning, as they passed by, they saw the fig tree dried up from the roots. And Peter calling to remembrance saith unto him, Master, behold, the fig tree which thou cursedst is withered away."*-Mark 11:20-21

> *"And Jesus answered and said unto it, No man eat fruit of thee hereafter for ever. And his disciples heard it."*- Mark 11:14

Jesus himself cursed the tree because it was the *beginning of sin.* Satan has used it to usher in sin. It was obvious that it covered its fruit and was not revealing fruit all year long. The fig tree was seen many times and always represented religion or (*covering up with our own means*) but Jesus would use an innocent lamb in Genesis, even though He could have used any material. Jesus was showing us yet another sign to come on the cross. The Bible makes what I believe (*based on scripture*) a clear case of the fig representing *Israel or religion.*

THE APPLE OR THE ALMOND?

There never was an apple mentioned in scripture! To begin with, apples are very high in sugar. I am not saying they are bad for you, I'm just saying vegetables appear to be healthier. Now that I have your attention using this silly analogy, let's get into it! Did Eve eat an apple? I have to build this analogy up to fully explain. Jesus is referenced to as a Branch many times in scripture:

> *"Every branch in me that beareth not fruit he taketh away: and every branch that beareth fruit, he purgeth it, that it may bring forth more fruit."*
> *"Abide in me, and I in you. As the <u>branch</u> cannot bear fruit of itself, except it abide in the vine; no more can ye, except ye abide in me. I am the vine, ye are the <u>branches:</u> He that abideth in me, and I in him, the same bringeth forth much fruit: for without me ye can do nothing."*-John 15:2,4-5

Jesus is the branch!

> *"Behold, the days come, saith the Lord, that I will raise unto David a <u>righteous Branch</u>, and a King shall reign and prosper, and shall execute judgment and justice in the earth."*-Jeremiah 23:5

"In that day shall the branch of the Lord be beautiful and glorious, and the fruit of the earth shall be excellent and comely for them that are escaped of Israel."-Isaiah 4:2

"And speak unto him, saying, Thus speaketh the Lord of hosts, saying, Behold the man whose name is The Branch; and he shall grow up out of his place, and he shall build the temple of the Lord:"-Zechariah 6:12

"Hear now, O Joshua the high priest, thou, and thy fellows that sit before thee: for they are men wondered at: for, behold, I will bring forth my servant the Branch."-Zechariah 3:8

"Yea, though I walk through the valley of the shadow of death, I will fear no evil: for thou art with me; thy rod and thy staff they comfort me."-Psalms 23:4

These scriptures reference so many places where Jesus is called *(ROD and STAFF.)* Let's move on to our final point. Moses is told in the wilderness to talk to the children of Israel as they are in the wilderness and took a rod to each family according to their house. There were *twelve* tribes camped out around the Tabernacle and wrote their names on them. They were told to lay them all by the Ark of the Covenant. God said He would meet them in the morning. He said whichever rod would bud in the morning, He would assign him as the high priest who would enter in the Holy of Holies once a year. Aaron's rod was the only rod or branch to bud and he was chosen. This is interesting for a few reasons. How would a branch cut off from life, still bud, unless this tree was life, *Hmmmmm?*

THE ALMOND ROD

I'll bet you're thinking, hmm how can it be a fruit? Well actually the almonds, oddly enough, grow quite heavily in the areas of Syria, Iran nowadays. *Almond fruit, That's right, it's a fruit!* They are actually the seed of the Almond fruit. Do you remember *"The Seed"* rule, that God made with seeds in Genesis when He said the seed would produce more of its own kind?

> *"And God said, Let the earth bring forth grass, the herb yielding seed, and the fruit tree yielding fruit after his kind, whose seed is in itself, upon the earth: and it was so."*- Genesis 1:11

BRANCH IS THE ALMOND ROD

The Almond tree is the first tree to bloom in the Spring and yield its fruit. With that being said, the word *almond* means, *"in a hurry."* *It was the first fruit in the Garden!*

> *"For if the firstfruit be holy, the lump is also holy: and if the root be holy, so are the <u>branches.</u>"*-Romans 11:16

Here we have a reference of the first fruit being holy and I know someone else who is Holy. *Jesus is Holy!* This also mentions *Branch,* and we have already determined that many times the word *Branche is* mentioned when describing Jesus. If the Tree of Life was the Tree of Life then I would suppose you couldn't kill it, which is just like Aaron's rod. *Hmmm?* There is another interesting thing to look at. The oldest name of Jerusalem is the name *(Luz.)* This means *(almonds.)* Jerusalem was named directly after almonds. In Jeremiah, it says…

> *"Moreover the word of the Lord came unto me, saying, Jeremiah, what seest thou? And I said, I see a rod of an almond tree. Then said the Lord*

unto me, Thou hast well seen: for I will hasten my word to perform it."- Jeremiah 1:11-12

The word *hasten* is used here or *"in a hurry!"* The truth is in the Word of God. *The first fruit would obviously be the Almond tree, which is the branch that has life on His own, and would have been the first fruit in the garden, which is obviously planted right from the beginning!*

JESUS IS CLEARLY THE BRANCH

I would venture to guess that Noah sent out that dove, and it came back with an *Olive branch,* and that it proved more than just life being out there! It was an *(olive branch)* from an *Olive tree.* That sounds a lot like a tree that you would find at the *Mount of Olives.* Guess where *Jesus* died and gave us new life? *Matthew 21 says it best!*

> *"And when they drew nigh unto Jerusalem, and were come to Bethphage, unto the <u>mount of Olives</u>, then sent Jesus two disciples,"*-Matthew 21:1

> *"For the wages of sin is death; but the gift of God is eternal life through Jesus Christ our Lord."*- Romans 6:23

> *"Christ hath redeemed us from the curse of the law, being made a curse for us: for it is written, Cursed is every one that hangeth on a tree:"*- Galatians 3:13

God has sanctified certain trees, or *wood.*

> *"Thou shalt have no other gods before me."*- Exodus 20:2

I'm pretty sure this includes all false idols that become our personal gods or belief systems or in my words, false religions. This leads me into our next topic, that I think will open your understanding even deeper. We are going to tackle one of most iconic religious misunderstood writings in the whole canon of the Bible!

THE TEN COMMANDMENTS

The Ten Commandments are widely misunderstood due to religious misteaching in churches all around the world. This has led to widespread hatred and misunderstanding towards the Christian community on a global level. The Bible has been divided into two parts . The *"Old Covenant"* contains the laws and the prophets as well as the Psalms of David and Proverbs and the *(New Covenant)* or promise, containing mainly the *four* Gospels and the letters to the churches and the Book of Revelation. The Ten commandments were given to Moses. Moses was considered to be the writer of which is called the *(Torah)* or the first *five* books during his wanderings in the wilderness. An interesting thing to note is when you get to the book of Joshua or *"salvation,"* He was also called Yeshua. The equivalent greek name would be *"Jesus."* *(originally meaning Hoshea)* you will see an actual parallel from the *Age of Law* and *Grace.* Moses goes up into Mount Sinai and is given commandment in stone.

> *"And the angel of the Lord appeared unto him in a flame of fire out of the midst of a bush: and he looked, and, behold, the bush burned with fire, and the bush was not consumed. "*-Exodus 3:2

Moses was given the order of the Priesthood, and blueprints in which the Tabernacle would be built. He was given the Laws of the Testimony *(The Ten Commandments)* which were written in stone by the finger of God Himself.

> *"And he gave unto Moses, when he had made an end of communing with him upon mount Sinai,*

two tables of testimony, tables of stone, written with the finger of God."-Exodus 31:18

These were laws written by God but they were made as moral laws because the people of that time had 613 laws to follow and it was impossible to fulfill them all. They were all caught up in religion. The commandments were set in place by God, who knew that the people could not keep the law, and if they would reflect on the commandments and realize that their law couldn't help them and only Jesus can.

When Jesus showed up on the scene in Matthew 5:17, He said this *"Think not that I am come to destroy the law, or the prophets: I am not come to destroy, but to fulfil."*

He was saying that I didn't come to destroy the Word that was given to Moses but *I AM* here to fulfill the scriptures which were written of Me! When the book of Joshua begins, it is said that *"-Moses is dead."*

> *"Moses my servant is dead; now therefore arise, go over this Jordan, thou, and all this people, unto the land which I do give to them, even to the children of Israel."*- Joshua 1:2

There is a parallel being drawn here and it is that Moses *(The Law Age)* is dead and Joshua, *(Grace and Truth,)* is coming through Jesus Christ! *"For the law was given by Moses, but grace and truth came by Jesus Christ."*- John 1:17

Stop being religious!

> *"Let every soul be subject unto the higher powers. For there is no power but of God: the powers that be are ordained of God. Whosoever therefore resisteth the power, resisteth the ordinance of God: and they that resist shall receive to*

themselves damnation. For rulers are not a terror to good works, but to the evil. Wilt thou then not be afraid of the power? do that which is good, and thou shalt have praise of the same: For he is the minister of God to thee for good. But if thou do that which is evil, be afraid; for he beareth not the sword in vain: for he is the minister of God, a revenger to execute wrath upon him that doeth evil. Wherefore ye must needs be subject, not only for wrath, but also for conscience sake. For for this cause pay ye tribute also: for they are God's ministers, attending continually upon this very thing. Render therefore to all their dues: tribute to whom tribute is due; custom to whom custom; fear to whom fear; honour to whom honour. Owe no man any thing, but to love one another: for he that loveth another hath fulfilled the law. For this, Thou shalt not commit adultery, Thou shalt not kill, Thou shalt not steal, Thou shalt not bear false witness, Thou shalt not covet; and if there be any other commandment, it is briefly compre-hended in this saying, namely, Thou shalt love thy neighbour as thyself. Love worketh no ill to his neighbour: therefore love is the fulfilling of the law. And that, knowing the time, that now it is high time to awake out of sleep: for now is our salvation nearer than when we believed. The night is far spent, the day is at hand: let us there-fore cast off the works of darkness, and let us put on the armour of light. Let us walk honestly, as in the day; not in rioting and drunkenness, not in chambering and wantonness, not in strife and envying. But put ye on the Lord Jesus Christ, and make not provision for the flesh, to fulfil the lusts thereof."- Romans 13:1-14

Chapter 11

GIFTS, PROPHECY, TONGUES, & TABERNACLE

IS MODERN DAY PROPHECY AND SPIRITUAL GIFTING A RELIGION ?

Proverbs 18:21 *"Words can destroy worlds."* Your words are weapons of mass destruction. We can heal from sticks but words spoil us from the inside out.

> *"But he that prophesieth speaketh unto men to edification, and exhortation, and comfort."*-1 Corinthians 14:3

Exhortation means that it exerts a moral law such as the Gospel, which we already have and have no need for a man to provide us! Let's take a moment to understand what determines prophecy. Prophecy was to be one hundred percent accurate at all times or the (*prophet or teller*) would have likely been stoned. Anyone who would have had a prophecy would have never spoken without absolute confidence with the fear of death! This is known generally as the foretelling of something to come. It is widely known that in the Old Testament there were several prophets, who would foretell the coming of our Lord and Savior, Jesus Christ. Keep in mind that the Old Testament was a testament with foretellers of the future according to God's revealing words. This brings me to the New Testament. The New Testament is a record of Jesus's birth and ministry.

> *"Beloved, believe not every spirit, but try the spirits whether they are of God: because many false prophets are gone out into the world."*- John 4:1

> *"God, who at sundry times and in divers manners spake in time past unto the fathers by the prophets,"* V.2 *"Hath in these last days spoken unto us by his Son, whom he hath appointed heir of all things, by whom also he made the worlds;"*-Hebrews 1:1-2

A prophet would have heard directly from God. Prophecy would have come from God Himself, not the avenue of direct will or preparation. (*Prophetic Reading/Dream Interpretations etc*) That is simply a religious act to mimic men of the Bible like Daniel, etc. God could have spoken for Himself through His Son, through the Holy Spirit and maintained His already perfect will through scriptures. Here's an example when Jesus is preaching during the Sermon on the Mount. He says…

> *"But I say unto you, That whosoever looketh on a woman to lust after her hath committed adultery with her already in his heart."*-*Matthew 5:28* or

> *"Think not that I am come to destroy the law, or the prophets: I am not come to destroy, but to fulfil."*-Matthew 5:17

You may ask why I bring this up? The reason I bring this to your attention is I'm sure there are many prosperity preachers today as well as (*spirit filled*) preacher's who will center their religion around a foreknown and summoned form of Spiritual Gifts. These people may go to the scripture and bring up the fact that so many people healed and prophesied in the Bible. As you search the scripture you will notice that this was obviously a deep rooted gift of those who lived before Jesus's birth. The point I'm making, concerning the book, is to make two things known. God's Word and His Spirit will *always* accompany one another. The Godhead, is the *Father, The Word and The Holy Ghost*, and are *never* separated. If one does not illuminate the other, then it cannot be true!

THE TABERNACLE

The time of the Old Covenant was considered the law age. This is the dispensation, or time period that God gave the law to Moses. Grace was given by Jesus Christ in the New Testament. Before Jesus was even born, the Israelites were bound by the laws that Moses received up in the mountain, in the wilderness.

> *"For the law was given by Moses, but grace and truth came by Jesus Christ."*- John 1:17

The wilderness was a place of death, heat and famine. The only original source of water was in Egypt. It wasn't until God sent water out of a rock.

> *"And the people thirsted there for water; and the people murmured against Moses, and said, Wherefore is this that thou hast brought us up out of Egypt, to kill us and our children and our cattle with thirst?" And Moses cried unto the Lord, saying, What shall I do unto this people? they be almost ready to stone me." And the Lord said unto Moses, Go on before the people, and take with thee of the elders of Israel; and thy rod, wherewith thou smotest the river, take in thine hand, and go." Behold, I will stand before thee there upon the rock in Horeb; and thou shalt*

smite the rock, and there shall come water out of it, that the people may drink. And Moses did so in the sight of the elders of Israel."- Exodus 17:3-6

The Israelites were so bound by religion, that they spent *forty* years in the wilderness trying to find the Holy Land when they could have been there much sooner. As the Israelites traveled through the desert they had no covering, except the *Tabernacle*. The Tabernacle would be transported and assembled by a specific group of people, *(the Levites carried The Ark of the Covenant)* and only Aaron was allowed to enter once a year. Aaron would enter into the Holy of Holies, to put innocent blood in *(seven markings)* on the top of the mercy seat. *(Interesting side note)* Jesus had seven markings on his body, *two* in the hands, *two* in His feet, cuts on His back, thorns on His head and a spear to the rib when He died. This was a religious practice that only the high priest was allowed to perform. It was believed that if anyone touched the Ark, or even looked at it, they would die. It is said that the high priest would have bells laced into their robe garnishes (which had a rope or chain attached) in case something went wrong. The idea was if the priest would enter the Holy of Holies, and the bells stopped moving, they would pull the priest out, so the priest wouldn't die.

In the Tabernacle diagram below, you will notice the *seven branch candlestick or Menorah.* On the left or *south* side of the Tabernacle, which has a light that stays lit at all times. The purpose is to reflect the *seven* anointings of the Holy Spirit, referenced in *Isaiah 11:2,* onto the Table of Shewbread on the right, which represents God's Word. *(This is symbolic of God's Anointing on His Word!)* As you enter the Tabernacle, before entering into the *Holy of Holies*, you would have The Illumination of the seven spirits mentioned in *Isaiah 11:2, which I will mention in the next chapter. (Chapter twelve)* On the right side of the tent was the table of the *Shewbread (God's Word)* representing the *(twelve Tribes of Israel, which I will list below.)* This is a picture of how a sinful man should come before a Holy God! This is a pattern that God has set up. *You cannot separate God's Word from His spirit!*

TWELVE TRIBES OF ISRAEL

1. Reuben	(Hebrew ראובן Rə'ûḇēn)
2. Simeon	(שמעון Šim'ôn)
3. Ephraim	(לוי Lêwî)
4. Judah	(יהודה Yehuḏā).
5. Issachar	(יששכר Yiśśāḵār).
6. Zebulun	(זבולון Zəḇūlun)
7. Dan	(דן Dān)
8. Naphtali	(נפתלי Naptālî).
9. Gad	(גד Gāḏ).
10. Asher	(אשר 'Āšêr)
11. Manasseh	(מנשה Mənaššeh)
12. Benjamin	(בנימין Binyāmîn).

THE OUTER COURTYARD

"Jesus saith unto him, I am the way, the truth, and the life: no man cometh unto the Father, but by me."- John 14:6

Jesus is saying *"I am Truth"* and *"The Word"* which is the table of Shewbread, on the right of the diagram. There are so many spiritual parallels within the Tabernacle. I will quickly lead you through some amazing pictures of Jesus in this section, but you must look for yourself. As you walk in the outer section of the courtyard, you will first first come into the Outer Court, which represents *(Thanksgiving)* or *(The Way.)* This area is illuminated by natural sunlight. You will notice in this section, the Bible says that everything is covered in brass or *(brazen)* which tends to always represent *(judgment.)* Satan is also called the *"brazen serpent."* *Thanksgiving* moves you closer to God.

"Because that, when they knew God, they glorified him not as God, neither were thankful; but

became vain in their imaginations, and their foolish heart was darkened."- Romans 1:21

"But love ye your enemies, and do good, and lend, hoping for nothing again; and your reward shall be great, and ye shall be the children of the Highest: for he is kind unto the unthankful and to the evil."- Luke 6:35

"Make a joyful noise unto the Lord, all ye lands. Serve the Lord with gladness: come before his presence with singing. Know ye that the Lord he is God: it is he that hath made us, and not we ourselves; we are his people, and the sheep of his pasture. Enter into his gates with (thanksgiving,) and into his courts with (praise): be thankful unto him, and bless his name. For the Lord is good; his (mercy) is everlasting; and his truth endureth to all generations."- Psalms 100:1-5

In the outer court you will come to the *(Brazen Altar #1), which is the first of seven different articles, before entering into God's Holy place.* It was made of wood and coated in brass because of the high temperatures. This is where sacrifices would happen first! Then you would come upon the *(brazen laver #2), which was a basin filled with water. This item was a place that the priest would wash his hands and see a reflection of himself before entering into the inner court. The Bible does not mention any dimensions. I believe that God gives no dimensions because there is no limit to who can wash their hands in His water before entering His covering.*

THE INNER COURT

The Inner Court represented (*Praise*) and (*The Truth.*) This section has to do with (*what you know.*) We are to give thanks because of what we have in the (*Outer Court*), but we praise upon what we know. The Inner Court is based upon the *knowledge of The Word of God* and His anointings. This part of the Tabernacle has the (*seven branch candlestick on the left #3*), or (*south*) and the Word, or (*Shewbread #4*) on the north or right side. The twelve loaves of shewbread are *unleavened or without sin. The bread had no yeast and was not "puffed up,"* and represented the twelve tribes of Israel or (*The Word.*) The seven branched candlestick on the left was made from one solid piece of gold, which had been beaten into shape. (*Jesus was also beaten*)

> *"And thou shalt make a candlestick of pure gold: of beaten work shall the candlestick be made: his shaft, and his branches, his bowls, his knops, and his flowers, shall be of the same."*- Exodus 25:31

This item had no dimensions. The lamp was lit with pure olive oil and was never to go out. The wic was typically provided by the tail of the Priest's garment. This article consisted of seven branches. The outer three branches, on each side had three separate almond blossoms, that were each made with three phases of an almond in bloom. The middle branch represented *"wisdom."* The center branch had four almond blossoms, and it too, had all *three* stages of the almond on it's individual branch. The center branch would total twelve. Each of the outer branches having *three* almonds, with their phases, would total *nine* on each branch, totaling *twenty seven* phases on either side of the center branch. This means *twenty seven* on the left and *twenty seven* on the right, and *twelve* in the middle. The grand total of almonds and their phases are sixty six. I find it very curious that the Bible lists *twelve* tribes, and *sixty six* books in the Bible! It's very interesting that there are *thirty nine* books in the Old Testament and *twenty seven* books in the New Testament. Oddly enough, if you were to remove *three* branches off of the right side, it would leave you with *thirty nine* almonds and their different phases, on the left and *twenty seven* on the right! *Do you see this picture*? This *seven* branch candlestick would clearly show a spiritual parallel. The Bible says that the center candle represents *wisdom* and it never goes out! This would show me that the anointing (*light*) from the Word of God would be the *only* light in the room, that would directly illuminate the bread or God's Word, on the right!

When the Israelites entered this section, they were no longer in natural sunlight. As you walked past the candlestick, and the bread, they would always be together. *The Holy Spirit and the Word cannot be separated!* The (*Golden Altar of Incense #5)* would be the last thing that you would see before entering the *Holy of Holies.* This is the place of praise. This was all about offering a sweet smelling aroma to God! This sweet fragrance would stay lit by the high priest. (*Aaron*) This would fill the tent before entering the Holy place. The altar was also coated in gold, and contained spices.

"And thou shalt make an altar to burn incense upon: of shittim wood shalt thou make it."- Exodus 30:1

THE HOLY OF HOLIES

The *Holy of Holies* represented the (*The Life*) *worship.* This is the place you no longer needed natural light (*Outer Court*) or the light from the candle (*Inner Court.*) This is the place where God dwells. As you look through the Book of Revelation you will notice *(the final kingdom.)*

> *"And I saw no temple therein: for the Lord God Almighty and the Lamb are the temple of it."-* Revelation 21:22

This room only needed God! The last two articles of this room were (*The Ark of the Covenant #6,)* and (*The Mercy Seat #7,)* on top of the Ark. This seat was made of *one hundred* percent pure gold, just as the candlestick was. There were two Cherubs on top of the Mercy Seat. These Cherubs were known to usher God in! I think it's interesting that the broken Commandments were on the inside of the Ark. When Jesus sat on it, (*with his innocent blood,)* God accepted His sacrifice, and cannot see our *"broken law"* underneath. We broke the law, and Jesus covered it! God is satisfied with what Jesus did! *God couldn't see our sin!*

This study goes so much deeper, but if you study the book of Exodus and Numbers, you will discover the diagram of the Tabernacle and the tribes camped outside like one giant picture of Jesus. The tribes were specifically laid out in a way that will paint a supernatural picture of Jesus! The four major camps on the outside of the Tabernacle are represented by the *four* Gospels! (*Matthew-Lion-Judah-camped East*) (*Mark-Ox-Manassa-camped West*) (*Luke-Man-Ruebin camped South*) and (*John-Eagle-Dan camped North*) *Take a look at this diagram and it will blow your mind!* This entire study is a giant picture of Jesus on the cross!!!

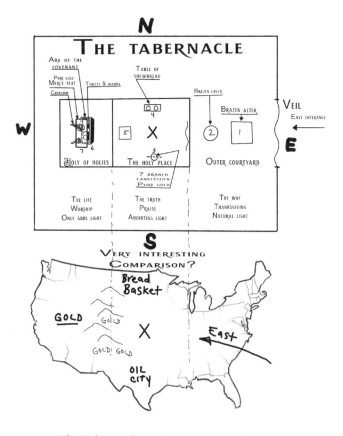

The Tabernacle and it's seven articles

> *"For there are three that bear record in heaven, the Father, the Word, and The Holy Ghost: and these three are one."*- 1 John 5:7

These cannot be separated! *ever*! Religious denominations often claim that you can have one, but not the other. If I were to claim to have an anointing of the Holy Spirit, and the Word does not align with it, then I am a liar and it should be completely ignored. Some versions (*as I have mentioned elsewhere in this book*) have omitted this verse. In other cases someone has changed the Words, *"These three are one"* to *"These three are In agreement."* One means *one*, and agreement means that they agree and have nothing to do with being *one!* Once again we have people altering God's Word to make other people happy or to sell more Bibles. God's original Word is to glorify Him alone! The Holy Spirit will reveal a false prophet to us!

> *"But if ye be led of the Spirit, ye are not under the law."*- Galatians 5:18

THE GIFT OF TONGUES ?

My intent in this section is not to offend anyone in the Pentecostal Religion or any other group. My intent here is to use scripture to reveal the truth, and specific customs adopted from things taught at home or in any religious groups. My hope for you is when you go into your prayer closest, you will delve into God's Word and hear from the Holy Spirit yourself, allowing Him to guide your understanding. It is my prayer that you search the scriptures entirely after reading this book and let the Bible reveal itself. Let's set this up... You may have heard certain denominations say that they have (*The gift of tongues*) or (*The Baptism of the Holy Ghost*) or (*Charismatics.*) This is widely known to be a gift required to get the *"Baptism of the Holy Spirit for salvation."* This reminds me of religion, even though God's Word gives us a clear definition of how to get into heaven in *John 3:16.*

The Apostle Luke begins to write the book of Acts, and it was written *(in regards to the Great Commission of Jesus Christ)* to share the Gospel, and to advance the kingdom of God to the uttermost parts of the world in the areas of Jerusalem, Judea and Samaria.

>*"But ye shall receive power, after that the Holy Ghost is come upon you: and ye shall be witnesses unto me both in Jerusalem, and in all Judaea, and in Samaria, and unto the uttermost part of the earth."*- Acts 1:8

>*"And if by grace, then is it no more of works: otherwise grace is no more grace. But if it be of works, then it is no more grace: otherwise work is no more work."*-Romans 11:6

>*"Though I speak with the <u>tongues of men</u> and of angels, and have <u>not</u> charity, I am become as sounding brass, or a tinkling cymbal."*-1 Corinthians 13:1-3

>*"but Israel, pursuing a law of righteousness, did not arrive at that law. Why? Because they did not pursue it by faith, but as though it were by works. They stumbled over the stumbling stone,"*-Romans 9:31-32

>*"who has saved us and called us with a holy calling, not according to our <u>works,</u> but according to His own purpose and grace which was granted us in Christ Jesus from all eternity,"*-2 Timothy 1:9

APOSTLE

(Latin Apostalus; Gr. To Send Away, To Sent.)-Noun

The Bible makes it very clear that God does not need our works. As we get to the books of Acts we see the actions of the Apostles. This section in the Bible has a lot to do with the beginning of the church and Apostles, who were also meeting in the upper room. It was written about the good news of our Lord and Savior *"Jesus Christ."* By this time, the Apostles had received the law of Moses.

According to the *1828 biblical dictionary, (Apostle)* means, *"A person deputed to execute some important business; but appropriately, a Disciple of Christ, commissioned to preach the gospel. Twelve persons were selected by Christ for this purpose;* and Judas, one of the number, proving an apostate, his place was supplied by Matthias in Acts 1:2. I often hear religious leaders refer to themselves as *Apostles* or *Reverends,* and these terms seem a bit unusual considering that there is only one man who is a true *King, Priest, Prophet, and Lord,* who is Himself the Apostle, Who is revered and worshipped. His name is *JESUS!*

The Apostles were to depart from Jerusalem and wait on the promise of their Father. They were told by Jesus that they would be baptized with the Holy Ghost not many days after his ascension into heaven, just as John the Baptist had baptized them.

> *"For John truly baptized with water; but ye shall be baptized with the Holy Ghost not many days hence."*-Acts 1:5

After leaving the mount of Olivet (*Olivet of Discourse*) V.3 of Acts reads:

> *"And when they were come in, they went up into an upper room, where abode both Peter, and James, and John, and Andrew, Philip, and Thomas, Bartholomew, and Matthew, James the son of Alphaeus, and Simon Zelotes, and Judas the brother of James."*-Acts 1:13

The apostles would go into prayer and it said the names were about 120.

> *"And in those days Peter stood up in the midst of the disciples, and said, (the number of names together were about an hundred and twenty,"*- Acts 1:15

Here is a side note about baptism (*of water and of the spirit.*) This is a widely known passage where Nicodemus comes to Jesus by night and they are talking, as Jesus explains to Nicodemus how to be born again. Jesus clearly tells Nicodemus that we must be born once by our mother's womb and a second time to enter into the kingdom of heaven.

> *"Jesus answered and said unto him, Verily, verily, I say unto thee, Except a man be born again, he cannot see the kingdom of God."*- John 3:3

In verse 4 Nicodemus asks...

> *"Nicodemus saith unto him, How can a man be born when he is old? can he enter the second time into his mother's womb, and be born?"*- John 3:4

Jesus states in verses 5-7,

> *"Jesus answered, Verily, verily, I say unto thee, Except a man be born of water and of the Spirit, he cannot enter into the kingdom of God. That which is born of the flesh is flesh; and that which is born of the Spirit is spirit. Marvel not that I said unto thee, Ye must be born again."*- John 3:5-7

This is a widely mistaught and misunderstood group of passages, that are very black and white. These statements can be cleared up with some simple study. Again, it is so easy to religiously just hear about these verses and assume Jesus is saying that it's required to be baptized in water to enter the kingdom of heaven. I've mentioned previously that the Word of God says *(by no works of man,)* can we enter the kingdom of Heaven. *John 3:16* explains it perfectly and explains how it's all about Jesus's *life, death and resurrection.* It's a matter of belief *on* what He did for us! Most religious people say that, *"I believe in God"* in which I would say, *(so does satan!)* Believing *in God* is a clearly different statement! This is to say that we believe upon the foundation of what He says and what He did. I believe in *(the evolutionary theory is taught)* but I *don't* believe in the information falsely taught about it. Let me ask you this, if a wedding band is removed, are you no longer married? *Of course you are!* Baptism is a perfect example of this. Baptism is just like the wedding band, because it is an outward proclamation of your bond with your spouse. It equally represents that you are in covenant and stand for one another, as well as what they represent. *"This is spiritual baptism!"*

DAY OF PENTECOST

Pentecost is *Greek for (Shavuot.)* This is the Israelites *spring harvest festival*. The festival got its name from the *50t*h day after Jesus's resurrection. *Penta* means *five,* because there are *five* books of the *Pentateuch.* On this day, according to Acts *2,* the apostles were all together and heard a mighty rushing wind that filled the place where they were sitting. The Bible says they spoke in *(cloven tongues.)*

> *"The apostles were all together "And when they were come in, they went up into an upper room, where abode both Peter, and James, and John, and Andrew, Philip, and Thomas, Bartholomew, and Matthew, James the son of Alphaeus, and Simon Zelotes, and Judas the brother of James. "*- Acts 2:1

V.2"And suddenly there came a sound from heaven as of a rushing mighty wind, and it filled all the house where they were sitting."

V.3"And there appeared unto them cloven tongues like as of fire, and it sat upon each of them."

V.4"And they were all filled with the Holy Ghost, and began to speak with other tongues, as the Spirit gave them utterances."

I believe that religion *way too often* has convinced certain religious groups to believe that they have been given some *"special gift,"* by God, that provides some *elite access to God.* I am not in any way saying that the Bible doesn't deal with this idea of tongues. I am simply saying that a relationship with Jesus is far simpler than religion has forced it to be! I'll explain further in just a moment, in the book of Corinthians. God has a lot to say about vain practices, and self edification as well as religious routine practices. He even says vain prayer is unexceptable.

"But when ye pray, use not vain repetitions, as the heathen do: for they think that they shall be heard for their much speaking."- Matthew 6:7

WHAT ARE TONGUES?

Tongues is an Old Testament Word, that is widely known to be supernatural God breathed utterances to those who are under the influence of some familiar spirits and chanting of mantras resembling foreign languages of some sort.

Tongues can be translated to its original Greek language by these words. *"Heteroglossia," "Dialektos"or "Glossa."* These words refer to a language, or *from the mouth.*

161

> *"And there appeared unto them cloven tongues like*
> *as of fire, and it sat upon each of them."-* Acts 2:3

It is interesting to note that this word is listed *sixteen* times and refers to *the mouth* or *organ of the mouth* and *thirty three* times, the word tongue is used to describe *languages of the world*. There is not one even one use or reference to this term, ever being used as some exciting and overwhelming force. I would venture to guess that the same Holy Spirit that I felt last Sunday during worship, was the same one that fell upon the disciples on that day. It was a miracle from God and it happened so that the disciples could spread the Good News of the Gospel to the whole world. Scripture goes on to say that (*16 different speaking nation leaders*) witnessed the Gospel in their own *tongue* or *known, spoken and received language!*

> *"Parthians, and Medes, and Elamites, and the*
> *dwellers in Mesopotamia, and in Judaea, and*
> *Cappadocia, in Pontus, and Asia, Phrygia, and*
> *Pamphylia, in Egypt, and in the parts of Libya*
> *about Cyrene, and strangers of Rome, Jews and*
> *proselytes, Cretes and Arabians, we do hear them*
> *speak in our tongues the wonderful works of*
> *God."-*Acts 2:9-11

The Bible has clearly identified that the apostles were Galilaens in vs 7, but the men listening heard the Gospel (*supernaturally*) in their own native (*language*) or *tongue!* Any reader can come to this conclusion (even with the facts I've brought to your attention,) and yes, you have complete free-will to do your own research. You also fully have the right to keep to your tradition. The Word of God clearly defines (*from what I read*) that it was not just some random sounds that were void of purpose!

> *"So shall my word be that goeth forth out of my*
> *mouth: it shall not return unto me void, but*
> *it shall accomplish that which I please, and it*

162

shall prosper in the thing whereto I sent it."-
Isaiah 55:11

If you're not convinced that man-made religion has caused us to
be misled, then let me take to 1 Corinthians. Here's another interesting fact... God first mentions in 1 Corinthians 12 (*Spiritual
gifts*) and in *1 Corinthians 13:14,* He outlines *love first,* and follows it up with *1 Corinthians 14:1-5*, and says this...

> *"Follow after charity, and desire spiritual gifts,
> but rather that ye may prophesy. For he that spea-
> keth in an unknown tongue speaketh not unto
> men, but unto God: for no man understandeth
> him; howbeit in the spirit he speaketh mysteries.
> But he that prophesieth speaketh unto men to edi-
> fication, and exhortation, and comfort. He that
> speaketh in an unknown tongue edifieth him-
> self; but he that prophesieth edifieth the church.
> I would that ye all spake with tongues but rather
> that ye prophesied: for greater is he that prophe-
> sieth than he that speaketh with tongues, except
> he interpret, that the church may receive edi-
> fying."*- Corinthians 14:1-5

*God is clearly saying here, after He defines love to "follow love,"
and desire spiritual gifts! It's better to prophesy or (preach) rather
than speak in an unknown (tongue) or unknown language.* It goes
on to say that if no one understands it, then it is just to edify and
glorify ourselves! *God is very clear here.*

> *"Now, brethren, if I come unto you <u>speaking with
> tongues,</u> what shall I profit you, except I shall
> speak to you either by revelation, or by knowl-
> edge, or by prophesying, or by doctrine? And even
> things without life giving sound, whether pipe or
> harp, except they give a distinction in the sounds,
> <u>how shall it be known what is piped or harped</u>?*

For if the trumpet give an uncertain sound, who shall prepare himself to the battle? So likewise ye, except ye utter by the tongue words easy to be understood, how shall it be known what is spoken? for ye shall speak into the air. There are, it may be, so many kinds of voices in the world, and none of them is without signification. Therefore if I know not the meaning of the voice, I shall be unto him that speaketh a barbarian, and he that speaketh shall be a barbarian unto me. Even so ye, forasmuch as ye are zealous of spiritual gifts, seek that ye may excel to the edifying of the church. "- 1 Corinthians 6:12

I think by this point, the Word of God makes it very clear. *Let's get back to relationships and not religion!* I'd like to use the *Classic Amplified Bible* to make this easier to receive. *"Though I speak with the tongues of <u>men</u> and of angels, and have not <u>charity</u>, I am become as sounding brass, or a tinkling cymbal V.2 "And though I have the gift of prophecy, and understand all mysteries, and all knowledge; and though I have all faith, so that I could remove mountains, and have not charity, I am nothing."- AMPC* 1 Corinthians 13:1

CAN ANYONE SEE GOD THROUGH DREAMS AND VISIONS?

I've heard several different accounts of people seeing angels or visions and all sorts of encounters. Don't let me try to change your mind. I know stories and experiences can seem extremely real and gather a listening audience. I'm sure someone will disagree with me, but our imaginations are very powerful, and our spiritual minds are created by God. For all I know, we see angels or a very filtered down version of God. If we can come down from our own prideful platform, we could learn the truth.

> *"Who only hath immortality, dwelling in the light which no man can approach unto; whom no man hath seen, nor can see: to whom be honour and power everlasting. Amen."*-1 Timothy 6:16

> *"No man hath seen God at any time, the only begotten Son, which is in the bosom of the Father, he hath declared him."*- John 1:18

I hate to break it to the religious crowd, but *only Jesus has truly seen the Father while still being in the form of flesh!*

> *"The fear of the Lord is the beginning of wisdom: and the knowledge of the holy is understanding."*- Proverbs 9:10

The word *fear is* translated from the Hebrew language. *Fear* is translated *"yir-aw"* or *"Morally Reverence."* We should reverence His Word!

> *"Trust in the Lord with all thine heart; and lean not unto thine own understanding. In all thy ways acknowledge him, and he shall direct thy paths. Be not wise in thine own eyes: fear the Lord, and depart from evil."*-Proverbs 3:5-7

Chapter 12

THE REVELATION NAMES AND THE HORSEMAN

THE REVELATION

The book of Revelation is widely misunderstood. It has been said that *the Old Testament is the New Testament concealed and the New Testament is the Old Testament revealed.* The word *Apocalypse* or *Greek* for "*apocalypsis*" simply means "*to disclose or unveiling or reveal.*"Religion has led us into believing that the Apocalypse is some scary Hollywood movie, but it simply means that something is being revealed! This is also where we get the word, "*Revelation,*"*not* Revelations! **This Is The Revelation Of Jesus Christ**! Did you catch that? *It's not the revelation of the antichrist!* The book of Revelation only mentions the antichrist, but it's not about him! So often you will hear preachers and pastors misteach or avoid this book altogether! *This is just like satan twisting the meaning of the Bible or convincing us not to read it at all!* Most people say"*It's so scary,*" or "*I don't understand it,*" or "*it's not about us because it's science fiction.*" It's for our learning and has a purpose! Of course satan wants us to avoid it, because it is dedicated to revealing Jesus Christ! Satan also knows that in the last chapters, his time is up. He knows that in the end, he's thrown into the lake of fire! He doesn't want you to know that, because if you did, you would pay more attention to the beginning of the Bible, and less time on him. The enemy knows if we were aware of his death, then it would build our faith from the very beginning!

> *"And I will put enmity between thee and the woman, and between thy seed and her seed; it shall bruise thy head, and thou shalt bruise his heel."*- Genesis 3:15

I'll discuss this further in a later portion of my book.

There is only *one* Revelation, and it's the Revelation of *JESUS CHRIST*! This entire book is about Jesus, *Himself.* This book is most likely written by the Apostle John, not John the Baptist. John wrote a total of five books, which are The Gospel of John, the three letters (*1,2 and 3rd John*) and the book of Revelation. The first line of the book states that it is *"The Revelation of Jesus Christ,"* and it is being given to Jesus *Himself,* to show His servants (*disciples.*) God signifies this revelation by His angels, to John (*the writer*) to record for us (*as John witnessed*) the whole thing. This book has *three* parts. They are:

The letter of Introduction, the seven letters to the seven churches of Asia, and the actual *prophecy,* which is the majority of the book.

In chapters 4-5, this book describes the throneroom of God very elaborately. As you advance to chapter *six*, you'll read about the four horsemen, which are misunderstood more often than not. As you work your way to the sixth chapter, you'll hear some Old Testament references. The references are about Someone who is able to open up a certain seven seals, and scrolls, who Is called *The Root of David* and *The Lion from the tribe of Judah*. John hears this but when he turns, he sees a bloody lamb. This *bloody lamb* (*Jesus*) begins to open these seven scrolls. I want to bring your attention to something. We have Jesus here, opening the scrolls and the Bible says that Jesus never bears witness of Himself.

> *"If I bear witness of myself, my witness is not true."*-John 5:31

We know based upon this truth and several others, that Jesus could not be referencing Himself. Religious people so often try to find contradictory flaws and mistakes in the Word of God, when in fact *there are no provable contractions*! The Bible is *always* consistent, cover to cover as long as we read and meditate daily on every word, and by doing so we will begin to see Jesus on every page!

This verse I've added as a little bonus verse to think about...

> **"Ye shall not add unto the word which I command you, neither shall ye diminish ought from it, that ye may keep the commandments of the Lord your God which I command you."**- Deuteronomy 4:2

THE TRUE 5TH HORSEMAN

Now we will take you to the *true horseman*. He is the *fifth* Horseman. *He is the True White Horseman!* He is the horseman who rolls in on the scene wearing many crowns and is followed by *many* white horsemen. *"His Name is called THE WORD OF GOD—JESUS CHRIST!"*

> *"And I saw heaven opened, and behold a white horse; and he that sat upon him was called Faithful and True, and in righteousness he doth judge and make war."*-Revelation 19:11

> *"And he was clothed with a vesture dipped in blood: and his name is called The Word of God."*-Revelation 19:13

If you read carefully, you will also notice that as the second, third and fourth horses are mentioned, they represent *death, destruction* and *war*, etc. As you read chapter *six,* when the first horseman shows up, he is (*promising peace and carrying a bow*) referencing the rainbow from Genesis, which was a promise that God would never flood the earth again!

> **"I do set my bow in the cloud, and it shall be for a token of a covenant between me and the earth."-** Genesis 9:13

> **"The Revelation of Jesus Christ, which God gave unto him, to shew unto his servants things which must shortly come to pass; and he sent and signified it by his angel unto his servant John:"-** Revelation 1:1

In verse *2* we read that John is to make a record of the Word of God, which is Jesus (*recorded in Revelation 19:13*) and testimony of Jesus.

> **"Who bare record of the word of God, and of the testimony of Jesus Christ, and of all things that he saw."-** Revelation 1:2

It's interesting to note that Jesus said in the book of Matthew, that satan would deceive us and we would hear of *wars, rumors of war, famines and pestilences*. You will always notice that Jesus is saying not to let anyone deceive us and they will come impersonating Him!

> **"And Jesus answered and said unto them, Take heed that no man deceive you. For many shall come in my name, saying, I am Christ; and shall deceive many. And ye shall hear of wars and rumours of wars: see that ye be not troubled: for all these things must come to pass, but**

the end is not yet. For nation shall rise against nation, and kingdom against kingdom: and there shall be famines, and pestilences, and earthquakes, in divers places. All these are the beginning of sorrows. Then shall they deliver you up to be afflicted, and shall kill you: and ye shall be hated of all nations for my name's sake. And then shall many be offended, and shall betray one another, and shall hate one another. And many false prophets shall rise, and shall deceive many."-Matthew 24:4-11

This brings two facts to my attention...

No 1.- Jesus wouldn't testify of Himself. He does *however,* always point people to the scripture about Himself, but He *never* testifies directly!

Here are a couple examples...

> *"Then said I, Lo, I come: in the volume of the book it is written of me,"*-Psalms 40:7

> *"Search the scriptures; for in them ye think ye have eternal life: and they are they which testify of me."*-John 5:39

> *"Then said I, Lo, I come (in the volume of the book it is written of me,) to do thy will, O God."*-Hebrews 10:7

No 2.- Why would our *Lord* or (*owner*) ride onto the scene hanging out with the worst people? (*Death, destruction and war*) He wouldn't, of course! By the way, He did spend time with *sinners, adulterers* and *tax collectors,* but those references were directed at people He was ministering to. He would never be (*in covenant*) in a battle against evil in this sense. *Jesus never takes the side of* *a sinner!* I said previously that conviction is when we take sides with God against our own sin!

> *"Thou therefore endure hardness, as a good soldier of Jesus Christ. No man that warreth entangleth himself with the affairs of this life; that he may please him who hath chosen him to be a soldier."*- 2 Timothy 2:3-4

> *"For I testify unto every man that heareth the words of the prophecy of this book, If any man shall add unto these things, God shall add unto him the plagues that are written in this book:"*- Revelation 22:18

> *"This book of the law shall not depart out of thy mouth; but thou shalt meditate therein day and night, that thou mayest observe to do according to all that is written therein: for then thou shalt make thy way prosperous, and then thou shalt have good success."*-Joshua 1:8

DID YOU KNOW THAT THERE ARE 7 BEATITUDES IN REVELATION?

> *"Blessed is he who reads and those who hear the words of the prophecy, and heed the things which are written in it; for the time is near."*- Revelation 1:1

> *"Blessed are the dead who die in the Lord from now on!"*- Revelation 1:3

> *"Blessed is the one who stays awake and keeps his clothes, so that he will not walk about naked and men see his shame"*-Revelation 14:13

"Blessed are those who are invited to the marriage supper of the Lamb"-Revelation 16:15

"Blessed and holy is the one who has a part in the first resurrection; over these the second death has no power, but they will be priests of God and of Christ and will reign with Him for a thousand years"- Revelation 19:9

"And behold, I am coming quickly. Blessed is he who heeds the words of the prophecy of this book"- Revelation 20:6

"Blessed are those who wash their robes, so that they may have the right to the tree of life, and may enter by the gates into the city"-Revelation 22:7,22:14

THE 7 ANOINTINGS OF THE LORD

"And the spirit of the Lord shall rest upon him, the spirit of wisdom and understanding, the spirit of counsel and might, the spirit of knowledge and of the fear of the Lord;"-Isaiah 11:2

1. *Spirit of the Lord*
2. *Spirit of Wisdom*
3. *Spirit of Understanding*
4. *Spirit of Council*
5. *Spirit of Might*
6. *Spirit of Knowledge*
7. *Spirit of the Fear of the Lord*

THE 9 FRUITS OF THE SPIRIT

"But the fruit of the Spirit is love, joy, peace, longsuffering, gentleness, goodness, faith, meekness, temperance: against such there is no law."-Galatians 5:22-23

1. *Love*
2. *Joy*
3. *Peace*
4. *Longsuffering*
5. *Gentleness*
6. *Goodness*
7. *Faith*
8. *Meekness*
9. *Temperance*

THE 17 WORKS OF THE FLESH OF GALATIANS 5:19-21

V.19"Now the works of the flesh are manifest, which are these; Adultery, fornication, uncleanness, lasciviousness, V.20 Idolatry, witchcraft, hatred, variance, emulations, wrath, strife, seditions, heresies, V.21 Envyings, murders, drunkenness, revellings, and such like: of the which I tell you before, as I have also told you in time past, that they which do such things shall not inherit the kingdom of God."-Galatians 5:19-21

1. *Adultery (violation of marriage bed)*
2. *Fornication (lewdness unmarried)(or married)*
3. *Uncleanness (filthy or foul)*
4. *Lasciviousness (looseness or lustful)*
5. *Idolatry (false gods)*

174

6.   *Witchcraft*

7.   *Hatred*

8.   *Variance (uncertain affinity)(Debate)(Strife)*

9.   *Emulations (comparison or catching UP)*

10. *Wrath*

11. *Strife*

12. *Seditions*

13. *Heresies*

14. *Envyings*

15. *Murders*

16. *Drunkenness*

17. *Revellings*

WHAT DOES IT MEAN TO HAVE TRUE CONVICTION?

"Conviction is when we take sides with God against our own sin."

THE 18 THINGS THAT WILL COME IN THE LAST DAYS

> *This know also, that in the last days perilous times shall come. For men shall be lovers of their own selves, covetous, boasters, proud, blasphemers, disobedient to parents, unthankful, unholy, Without natural affection, trucebreakers, false accusers, incontinent, fierce, despisers of those that are good, Traitors, heady, highminded, lovers of pleasures more than lovers of God; Having a form of godliness, but denying the power thereof: from such turn away. For of this sort are they which creep into houses, and lead captive silly women laden with sins, led away with divers lusts, Ever learning, and never able to come to the knowledge of the truth."*-2 Timothy 3:1-7

1.   *Men shall be lovers of themselves*

2.   *Covetous*

3.   *Boasters*

4.   *Proud*

5.   *Blasphemers*

6.   *Disobedient to parents*

7.   *Unthankful*

8.   *Unholy*

9.   *Without Natural Affection*

10. *Trucebreakers*

11. *False Accusers*

12. *Incontinent*

13. *Fierce*

14. *Despisers of those that are good*

15. *Traitors*

16. *Heady*

17. *Highminded*

18. *Lovers of pleasures more than lovers of God*

19. *Having a form of Godliness, but denying the power thereof*

THE MANY NAMES OF GOD

God reveals Himself in many ways, and has names in which He expresses His manifested Glory. An example of this would be the first references in the book of Genesis.

> *"And Abraham called the name of that place Jehovahjireh: as it is said to this day, In the mount of the Lord it shall be seen." So something is being shown to us, that we are supposed to see!"*- Genesis 22:14

This leads me into our next subject…

What I'm about to say, will build your faith in a way that you will never see the Word of God the same ever again! It's funny that God would have the first mention of His name *(Jehovah,)* meaning *"The Revealing God" or "God revealed"* until now. *Here are some names of Jehovah.*

I. Advocate	I John 2: I
2. Lamb of God	John 1:29
3. The Resurrection, and the life	John 11:25
4. Shepherd Bishop of souls	1 Peter 2:25
5. Judge of the quick and the dead	Acts 10:42
6. Lord of lords	l Timothy 6:15
7. Man of sorrows	Isaiah 53:3
8. Head of the Church	Ephesians 5:23
9. Master	Matthew 8:19
10. Faithful and True Witness	Revelation 3:14
11. Rock	l Corinthians 10:4
12. High Priest	Hebrews 6:20
13. The Door	John 10:9
14, Living Water	John 4:10
15. Bread of Life	John 6:35
16. Rose of Sharon	Song of Solomon 2:I
17. Alpha & Omega	Revelation 22:13
18. True vine	John 15: I
19. Messiah	Daniel 9:25
20. Teacher	John 3:2
21. Holy One	Mark 1:24
22. Mediator	1 Timothy:2:5
23. THE Beloved	Ephesians 1:6
24. The Branch	Isaiah 11:1
25. Carpenter	Mark 6:13
26. Good Shepherd	John 10:11
27. Light of the World	John 8:12
28. Image of the Invisible God	Colossians 1:15

29. The Word	John 1:1
30. Chief Cornerstone	Ephesians 2:20
31. Savior	John 4:42
32. Servant	Matthew 12:18
33. Author and finisher of our faith	Hebrews 12.2
34. The Almighty	Revelation 1:8
35. Everlasting Father	Isaiah 9:6
36. Shiloh	Genesis 49:10
37. Lion of the Tribe of Judah	Revelation 5:5
38. I AM	John 8:58
39. King of kings	I Timothy 6:15
40. Prince of Peace	Isaiah 9:6
41. Bridegroom	Matthew 9:15
42. Only Begotten Son	John 3:16
43. Wonderful Counselor	Isaiah 9:6
44. Immanuel	Matthew 1:23
45. Son of Man	Matthew 20:28
46. Son of God	Mark 1:1
47. Dayspring	Luke 1:78
48. The Amen	Revelation 3:14
49. The First & the Last	Revelation 1:17

NAMES OF JEHOVAH "THE REVEALING GOD!"

1. *El De'ot (The God Of Knowledge) (1 Samuel 2:3)*

2. *El Emet (The God Of Truth) (Psalm 31:6)*

3. *El Yeshuati (The God Of My Salvation) (Isaiah 12:2)*

4. *El Elyon (The Most High God) (Genesis 14:18)*

5. *Immanu El (God Is With Us) (Isaiah 7:14)*

6. *Jehovah Shammah (The Lord is There)*

7. *Jehovah-Raah (The Lord My Shepherd)*

8. *Jehovah Rapha (The Lord That Heals)*

9. *Jehovah Nissi (the Lord our Banner)*

10. *Jehovah Shalom (God my peace)*

11. *Jehovah Tsidkenu (The Lord Our Righteousness)*

12. *Jehovah Mekoddishkem (The Lord Who Sanctifies You)*

13. *Jehovah Jireh (My Provider)*

14. *Elah Yerush'lem (God of Jerusalem) (Ezra 7:19)*

15. *Elah Yisrael (God of Israel) (Ezra 5:1)*

16. *Elah Sh'maya (God of Heaven) (Ezra 7:23)*

17. *Elah Sh'maya V'Arah (God of Heaven and Earth) (Ezra 5:11)*

18. *YHVH Elohim (LORD God) (Genesis 2:4)*

19. *YHVH M'kaddesh (The LORD Who Makes Holy) (Ezekiel 37:28)*

20. *YHVH Yireh (The LORD Who Sees/provides) (Genesis 22:14)*

21. *YHVH Nissi (The LORD My Banner) (Exodus 17:15)*

22. *YHVH Shalom (The LORD Of Peace) (Judges 6:24)*

23. *YHVH Tsidkenu (The LORD Our Righteousness) (Jeremiah 33:16)*

24. *Elohei Ma'uzzi (The God of my strength) (2 Sam 22:23)*

25. *Elohei Mikarov (The God who is near) (Jer 23:23)*

26. *Jehovah Jireh (The Lord Will Provide)*

27. *Jehovah Shalom (The Lord Is Peace)*

28. *Jehovah Sabaoth (The Lord of Hosts)*

29. *Yhwh Elohe Ƶeba'ot (Yhwh God of Hosts) or (God of Hosts)*

30. *Elohei Chasdi (The God of my kindness) (Ps 59:17)*

31. *Elohei Haelohim (The God of gods) (Josh 22:22)*

32. *Elohei Marom (The God of heights)(Micah 6:6)*

33. *Elohei Tzva'ot (The God of Hosts) (2 Sam 5:10)*

34. *Elohei Kedem (The Eternal God) (Deut 33:27)*

35. *Elohei Tehillati (The God of my praise) (Psalm 109:1)*

36. *Elohei Avoteinu (The God of our fathers) (Deut 26:1)*

37. *Elohim Avinu (God our Father)*

38. *Elohim Bashamayim (God in heaven)(2 Chron 20:6)*

39. *Elohim Chayim (The Living God) (Jos 3:10)*

40. *Elohei HaChayim (The God of the Living) (Mk 12:27)*

41. *Elohei haricot l'chol-basar (The God of the spirits of all flesh) (Num 16:22)*

42. *Elohim HaAv (God the Father) (Gal 1:1)*

43. *Elohim Emet (The God of truth) (Jere 10:10)*

44. *Adonai Yir'eh (The Lord who sees) (Gen 22:14)*

BIBLICAL NUMBERS

Numbers have a very important role in the Word of God. The original Hebrew that I previously mentioned in the (*Aleph Tav section of the book,*) indicated as to how God placed Himself throughout the scripture, into His Word. The Bible is filled from front to back with *numbers, types* and *shadows*, that help to reveal His plan of redemption for us. God likes numbers so much, in fact, He has woven numbers into the architect of the Tabernacle, the Ark and the Temple, and many other areas throughout the canon of the Bible. There are many signs of integrated design on every single page of the Bible. The Hebrew language itself uses numbers identified with letters. For example:

The letter representing *(Aleph)* is *(א)*, has a number value of (*1*) as well as words associated, such as **(*strength, service or God*)**. Another example is (***Tau or Tav***) (**ת**) represents the number (*400*) or (***mark, covenant, or destination***). These numbers are assigned to all of the (*22*) alphabet, and every Hebrew letter has a number assigned to each letter. Hebrew is so fascinating, because when you spell a pictographic word in Hebrew, the numbers associated with its corresponding letters (*individually*) add up to a number that has a meaning in itself! This language has so much meaning, that even a super computer could not calculate its vast supernatural implications and principles. I've made a lot of powerful statements, that would take me years to even come close to doing them justice. *I highly recommend that you do your own homework! You will find that there is a blessing hidden within its treasures!* Here is a simple list of numbers *(1-10)*, and their meanings. Below I will include the 22 letter Hebrew alphabet and its numerical value.

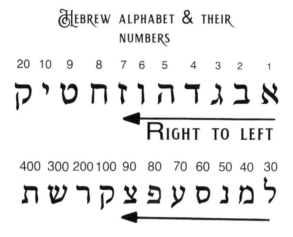

Hebrew alphabet and number values associated to them

Numbers (1-10)

#1—-God

#2—-in agreement or unity

#3—-whole or complete

#4—-earth or What's In Earth (4th Commandment, 4 Seasons, 4 Elements, 4 Directions, 4 Gospels, 4 Tribes, 4 Rivers In Genesis, 4th Clause In The Lord's Prayer Etc.)

#5—-grace

#6—-number of man or his image

#7—-wholeness

#8—-new Beginning or (s)

#9—-judgment

SCRIPTURE EXAMPLE OF NUMBERS

Matthew 5:3- *"Blessed are the poor in spirit: for theirs is the kingdom of heaven."*

Matthew 5:4- *"Blessed are they that mourn: for they shall be comforted."*

Matthew 5:5- *"Blessed are the meek: for they shall inherit the earth."*

Matthew 5:6- *"Blessed are they which do hunger and thirst after righteousness: for they shall be filled."*

Matthew 5:7- *"Blessed are the merciful: for they shall obtain mercy."*

Matthew 5:8- *"Blessed are the pure in heart: for they shall see God."*

Matthew 5:9- *"Blessed are the peacemakers: for they shall be called the children of God."*

Matthew 5:10- *"Blessed are they which are persecuted for righteousness' sake: for theirs is the kingdom of heaven."*

Matthew 5:11- *"Blessed are ye, when men shall revile you, and persecute you, and shall say all manner of evil against you falsely, for my sake."*

Here are other examples of significant symbolic numbers divisible by their root number.

(No.40) Jesus fasted 40 days and 40 nights in the desert. 40 days from Jesus's resurrection and His ascension. 40 days and nights Noah was at sea. Moses was in Egypt 40 years. Moses was 40 days and nights in Mt. Sainai. There were spoils and spies in Canaan for 40 days. David and Solomon reigned over Israel for 40 years.

(No.50) Pentecost was 50 days after Jesus's death and resurrection. The 50 days of Jubilee. In the law, the feast of Shavuot was 50 after passover or (*new harvest*).

(No 7) There were 7 days of creation, 7 good years and bad years of famine in Egypt. Hebrew slaves were set free in the 7th year. There are 7 feasts for the Lord. There are 7 days for each of the 2 main feasts. 7 priests with 7 trumpets when ahead for 7 days. Israel marched 7 times around Jericho. *The number 7 is everywhere in the book of Revelation.* There are ; 7 churches,7 spirits before the throne, 7 gold lampstands, 7 stars, 7 trumpets, 7 bowls, 7 seals, 7 angels of church, 7 horns, 7 Golden bowls, 7 torches, 7 thunders, 7 headed dragon, 7 crowns, 7 plagues, and 7 expressions of "blessed is", which I have listed in later chapters of this book.

(No 8) Jewish males circumcised on the 8th day old. 8 follows 7, Jesus rose on the 8th after the Sabbath,

(No 12) There are 12 tribes, 12 loaves of bread in the Tabernacle, 12 Apostles, 12 stones, and 12 gates, 12 pearls, mentioned in the kingdom of Revelation.

> *"And the twelve gates were twelve pearls: every several gate was of one pearl: and the street of the city was pure gold, as it were transparent glass."* - Revelation 21:21

In vs 22 its mentions that in this kingdom there was no except the lamb. Revelation 21:22 *"And I saw no temple therein: for the Lord God Almighty and the Lamb are the temple of it."*

(*No 10*) This is the number of the 10 virgins parable,10 Commandments, 10 Kingdoms, 10 plagues, etc.

(*No 3*) There are 3 parts(*Father, Son & Holy Spirit,*) 3 gifts-,(*Abraham, Isaiah, Jacob*)(*Peter, James and John*), (*1 John 5:7-"3 that testify"*)

Chapter 13

YES, 13 *MYTHS*

WHY IS 13 SO SCARY?

Have you ever been told that the number 13 is scary? The number 13 has several different legends and superstitions pertaining to its, *"do and don'ts."* One of the most widely rumored stories is the number 13 is (*Friday the 13th,*) which is believed to be when Jesus died on the cross. I should mention first (*as I will describe later in this chapter*) based on the Jewish calendar, Jesus would have clearly died on a *Wednesday*. On the other hand, the majority of people believe this is a reflection of Judas Escariot betraying, and selling out Jesus, after breaking bread with Him. Judas was known as the (*trader*) at the last supper with Jesus. Judas sold out Jesus for thirty Shekels of silver, and betrayed Him with a kiss.

> *"And he that betrayed him had given them a token, saying, Whomsoever I shall kiss, that same is he; take him, and lead him away safely."*-Mark 14:44

This has been a mythical belief that has caused so many people to fear silly fables through the years. Many people believe that *666* is some scary number of satan. *"The beast"* or that the number *13* has some supernatural connotation. Satan attempts to put fear in the hearts of people. *This is ultimately why religion is so dangerous!* There is actually a (*666*) condition known as (*hexakosioihexekontahexaphobia*.) Many religious conspiracy theorists believe that the antichrist is *Nero Caesar or Hitler* and several others.

ASTROLOGY

These are a few different religious practices:(Transcendental Meditation, yoga, oriental mysticism, devotionals, card reading, signs of the zodiac.) Besides the signs that are referenced in the Bible, God gives us knowledge through the Holy Spirit. The Bible does have mysteries within the stars, but *He never needs our worldly help! God doesn't need some spiritual act that makes us God! but rather He is God!* He will give us knowledge on His own. The Bible warns us of getting involved in pagen practices! Take a look at these scriptures, and how God uses the signs of heaven.

> *"And he brought him forth abroad, and said, Look now toward heaven, and tell the <u>stars</u>, if thou be able to number them: and he said unto him, So shall thy seed be."*- Genesis 15:5

> *"And God said, Let there be lights in the firmament of the heaven to divide the day from the night; and let them be for signs, and for seasons, and for days, and years:"*- Genesis 1:14

> *"Now when Jesus was born in Bethlehem of Judaea in the days of Herod the king, behold, there came wise men from the east to Jerusalem, Saying, Where is he that is born King of the Jews? for we have seen his star in the east, and are come to worship him."*- Matthew 2:1,2

"And there appeared a great wonder in heaven; a woman clothed with the sun, and the moon under her feet, and upon her head a crown of twelve stars:"- Revelation 12:1

I'd like to note the 1st Commandment in the Bible... **"Thou shalt have no other gods before me."**

I'm pretty sure this includes all false idols that become our personal gods or belief systems. *So what about false religions?* This leads me into our next topic. I think it will open your understanding even deeper.

BABY IN THE MANGER?

Was Jesus really a baby? *Maybe not.* There is a common misconception that the wise men visited Jesus on the night of His birth. The wiseman *could* have come years later. As a matter of fact in this verse, it says...

"And when they were come into the house"- Matthew 2:11

Jesus is not mentioned here in a stable, but a house. Jesus was visited after King Herod sent out for the murder of all two year males and below, after hearing that there was a coming king. He was looking for Jesus, so Joseph and Mary took Jesus away until after Herod was dead. Jesus is at least two years of age before the wisemen showed up offering Him gifts. *He could not have been a little baby! The Bible clearly focuses on Jesus's ministry as an adult!* The manger scenes are pretty, but have no real accuracy. I could go into much more detail but for the sake of this book, I urge you to do a little research on your own!

THREE CROSSES AT CALVARY?

The Bible does _not_ state there were _three_ crosses (_although it could very well be_) and wood was very hard to come by in the region. Old trees were used over and over and would have typically been bloody and reused. As a matter of fact, Jesus would likely have been tired and physically drained from being beaten, starved and kept up all night. It seems odd that He would be having a conversation from cross to cross with the other two criminals, while yelling. _It's very likely they were all hanging on one tree! The bible does not specify!_ It's also interesting to note that when the Roman soldiers walked to the men to break their legs, they would have walked right past Jesus, who was (_according to scripture_) in the middle. Why would they have walked past him without doing the same to Jesus? Was it because He was hung from a circular tree off to one side? Possibly, but I am not saying He was. I'm saying that it might have been a possibility! We should use true knowledge of scripture (_in its entirety_) to come to a conclusion. If you walked into a room and your wife was explaining how handsome this other man was, and you didn't hear the whole phone call, then how would you determine the context of the person spoken of? You wouldn't have enough information about the subject, because you didn't realize that she was complimenting her brother's wedding photos. You have then taken a few lines of text and applied it to your own conclusion. _This is the problem today!_

"And one of the malefactors which were hanged railed on him, saying, If thou be Christ, save thyself and us."-Luke 23:9

TOPICAL_VIEW

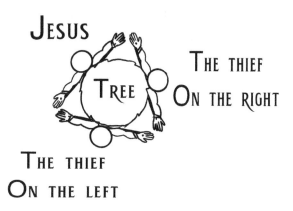

The Bible only says two thieves.

"Then were there two thieves crucified with him, one on the right hand, and another on the left"-Matthew 27:38

THE BLACK CAT LIE

According to one legend, this myth originally started in Egypt around *3000 BC*. Black cats were supposedly the rock stars of that time period and were considered to be in high esteem and to kill one was considered a capital crime! In the middle ages in Europe, they lost their status because they were beginning to be associated with so-called (*witches*) practicing black magic. The black magic practices were all the rage and soon would attract the attention of the Europians. These *Alley cats* were often cared for by old ladies. The old women would later be accused of witchery. An old folklore in the *1560* caught wind of it and the rumors spread throughout the area. Supposedly a father and son living in Lincolnshire were traveling and a black cat crossed their path. They dove into a crawl space and threw rocks at it until it ran into a woman's house, who was, at the time, suspected of being a witch. The next day the father and son came across the same woman and noticed that she was bruised and limping. They didn't believe it was a coincidence. After this, it became known that at nighttime, the old woman could turn herself into a cat. This belief would become common during the Salem witch hunt, and would become a practice still today, during Halloween. Some people now see the cat as prosperity. *Now for the truth!*

> *"For we have not followed cunningly devised fables, when we made known unto you the power and coming of our Lord Jesus Christ, but were eyewitnesses of his majesty."*-2 Peter 1:16

This is a product of the gatekeepers! The gatekeepers are the people who control the flow of information. *This entire story is ridiculous!* This story, among so many others, have helped to influence and massively flood the minds of so many. Satan will always use fear to control us. If we are in bondage to a myth or a religion, then he becomes the gatekeeper of your soul. Satan wants us to fear everything, but the Bible says *"perfect love casts out fear."* *We cannot love and fear at the same time! If fear becomes present, then love takes a back seat!*

> *"There is no fear in love; but perfect love casteth out fear: because fear hath torment. He that feareth is not made perfect in love."*- 1 John 4:18

This is the reason why we would run out into the street to save our children from being hit by an oncoming car. We just react with love, because fear has no power! When we fear, we have no room to love.

> *"Therefore take no thought, saying, What shall we eat? or What shall we drink? or, Wherewithal shall we be clothed? (For after all these things do the Gentiles seek:) for your heavenly Father*

> *knoweth that ye have need of all these things. But seek ye first the kingdom of God, and his righteousness; and all these things shall be added unto you. Take therefore no thought for the morrow: for the morrow shall take thought for the things of itself. Sufficient unto the day is the evil thereof.*"- Matthew 6:31-34

> *"No man can serve two masters: for either he will hate the one, and love the other; or else he will hold to the one, and despise the other. Ye cannot serve God and mammon.*"- Matthew 6:24

Mammon is rooted from the Greek word (*hammon.*) This is the love of more, as if trusting God and loving, instead of fearing. *We cannot not serve fear if we are serving God!* Love is the same way. If we are afraid, we are not able to fully love. *Let God be our constant and disregard man- made religious tales!*

FAITH OF A MUSTARD SEED?

This is a commonly misunderstood scripture...

> *"And Jesus said unto them, Because of your unbelief: for verily I say unto you, If ye have faith <u>as</u> a mustard seed, ye shall say unto this mountain, Remove hence to yonder place; and it shall remove; and nothing shall be impossible unto you.*"- Matthew 17:20

Jesus is <u>not</u> saying, *"oh I guess all you need is a tiny bit of faith, or (faith of).* Jesus says *"as" a mustard seed, which is entirely different. He is saying have faith* <u>just like</u> the tiny mustard seed. If you take the time to research a mustard seed, you will learn that they grow in virtually *any* environment. It could be raining or dry or under a rock; basically in any imaginable condition, and the seed will prevail, no matter how suppressed or against all opposition. Jesus is saying the word *"as"* a mustard seed, not *(of)* a mustard seed, to tell the reader to have *"extraordinary"* faith no matter the situation. *Not just some weak little faith!*

MOTHER MARY?

Yes, she is the mother of the flesh and body of Jesus, but did Mary give birth to God, who made her? Of course not! The Bible says Mary was preferred, but it says nothing about her being divine. Let's take a look…

> *"Therefore the Lord himself shall give you a sign; Behold, a virgin shall conceive, and bear a son, and shall call his name Immanuel."*-Isaiah 7:14

Immanuel means "God with us!"

> *"And the angel came in unto her, and said, Hail, thou that art highly <u>favoured</u>, the Lord is with thee: blessed art thou among women."*- Luke 1:28

Besides the King James Version, you will notice some dramatic differences from other Bibles. Here is what I *don't* see… *divinity!* Mary was obviously a good mother for the human baby Jesus *(flesh and blood baby.)* God wrapped himself in the human form of *(flesh and blood)* in *John 1:1-14*. Mary may have been a kind woman, but we have one saviour to worship. Based on the Bible that I read, and His name is *Jesus*.

IF ITS MY TIME, IT'S MY TIME

Wrong! You will often come across that person who says *"If the tornado hits me, it will hit me."* or, *"It is what it is!"* Let me show you what the scripture says about this matter.

"Be not over much wicked, neither be thou foolish: why shouldest thou die before thy time?"-Ecclesiastes 7:17

It is very clear in this passage that we have an appointed time and God knows it. God is saying *don't be a fool, (in my words)* why should you die early?..there it is! ***Free will***! Check out this verse...

"For I know the thoughts that I think toward you, saith the Lord, thoughts of peace, and not of evil, to give you an expected end.- Jeremiah 29:19

I referenced elsewhere in this book that God knows our expected end, but He loves us enough to allow us free will to affect it. *(other than natural death)*

"I call heaven and earth to record this day against you, that I have set before you life and death, blessing and cursing: therefore choose life, that both thou and thy seed may live:"- Deuteronomy 30:19

God's message is more than clear. He says, call heaven and earth against you or this is already known and recorded in heaven, and I have already scheduled or planned your day of birth and death; and you and all of your descendants. This means to me that God knows our end and has it ordained and recorded, enforcing a blessing and cursing based upon this. *This allows us to let him bring about our death naturally!* He is clear on the fact that He has blessings or curses already known and we should not alter it or it can change our outcome. His plans are better than ours. We clearly cannot affect natural life or death but we can alter early death, which affects the nation because of it.

CHRISTMAS IS *NOT* JESUS'S BIRTHDAY!

This may surprise you. *Jesus was not born on December 25th.* This date was announced and determined by the early church fathers, and was first mentioned in the (*Calender of Phiocaulus in 354 A.D.*) It was assumed that Jesus's birth was on a Friday, in *1 A.D. This is incorrect.* People of this time practiced Pegan rituals, which lured them into *Christian trappings*, and their beliefs were then *re-assembled & packaged.* Eventually, December 25th was adopted, and proclaimed by the church fathers in *440 A.D.*

There are many references that help to mathematically figure out Jesus's (*general*) birth but for the sake of this book I will keep it simple. We read about John the Baptist, who was the person who mentions Jesus's first appearance on earth, which gives us more information.

> *"There was a man sent from God, whose name was John."* (Vs7)*"The same came for a witness, to bear witness of the Light, that all men through him might believe."*- John 1:6-7

By using a few facts around Zacharias"(*John's Father*) and the birth of John, which was *April 19-20, 2 B.C.* The Bible says that John was *sex to eight* months older than Jesus which would put Jesus's birth around autumn. There are a few different possibilities, but my point is Jesus would have been born sometime between September and October, not December! This study has quite a bit more biblical chronology that I'm not spending much time on. The point I'm making is Jesus wasn't born on December 25th.

THREE WISE MEN?

Not necessarily. The Bible clearly states in Matthew 2:11...

> *"And when they were come into the house, they saw the young child with Mary his mother, and*

194

fell down, and worshipped him: and when they had opened their treasures, they presented unto him gifts; gold, frankincense and myrrh?"-
John 1:6-7

In V.*7* and V.*8* of Matthew Chapter *2,* King Herod heard about this King Jesus character, and when he called them in to send them out, there wasn't any mention of __any__ number of men at all, and *only* mentions *three* gifts that were given. Based upon the area of Iraq, and it's customary attributes of the day. This is a good idea of how Jesus *could* have looked. Please know that I am not saying this is how Jesus looked. My objective is to make you aware of the fact that we too often form an opinion from a religious stand-point! Religions become so intertwined into our heads that we begin forming pictures based upon what a man has told us, rather than focusing on what the bible says!

WAS JESUS THE HANDSOME PAINTING ON YOUR WALL?

Often we see so many pictures painted of Jesus in our *Western mentality*. We imagine Jesus as this light skinned blond haired model, who wears longing flowing white robes, but I hate to break it to you, there are a lot of things to consider before coming to this religious conclusion. The Bible says a lot of contrary statements opposing this idea, but you first have to *search the scriptures*! If you look today in the same general area of Iraq, you would most likely find darker complected men, as compared to the generally lighter skinned man here in the Western regions. Our western American self-centered view of Jesus, overlooks biblical archae-ology, as well as hereditcal, and doctrinal truths. We as a nation, are self-centered in our world view and think *we* are the center of the world! *We think it's all about us!* As a matter of fact, there isn't even one reference (*confirmed*) proving the United States even being referenced in the King James Bible. The book of Zechariah, which means,*"God remembers,"* says this:

> *"For thus saith the Lord of Hosts; After the glory hath he sent me unto the nations which spoiled you: for he that toucheth you toucheth the apple of his eye" the Bible references Israel as the Apple of God's eye!"*- Zechariah 2:8

Jesus was often commemorated by Greek statues. These early statues had long flowing hair and beautiful features! (*They were generally depicted in ancient Zeus stone statues.*) It was often thought that Jesus was the son of the Greek God. Many paintings were created and adopted during this time period. Most of the images we adopt and pass down, and would have wealthy stigmas attached to them. Most paintings of Jesus, pictured stakes pierced through the front of His feet, upon a wooden block, neither of which are in the Bible. It's more likely, (*based upon the fact that the Romans were experts in the art of crucifixion,*) they would have put the stakes through the side of the Achilles heel. *Please do your own research, in regards to crucifixions, and how they were performed.* The point here isn't to convince you of anything that I've written. I'm more concerned that you take the time and research for yourself, rather than assuming religious ideas that you may have seen in paintings!

> *"And he said unto them in his doctrine, Beware of the scribes, which love to go in long clothing, and love salutations in the marketplace, V39-And the chief seats in the synagogues, and the uppermost rooms at feasts:"*- Mark 12: 38-39

Here we have Jesus warning us about long fancy robes (*royalty*) etc. This by itself, suggests that Jesus was not a fan of fancy looking attire that would edify oneself. Jesus wasn't really described (*in detail*) in the Gospels, most likely because He was very average looking. We do have some scriptures that give us some idea of His lack *of looks.*

"But the Lord said unto Samuel, Look not on his countenance, or on the height of his stature; because I have refused him: for the Lord seeth not as man seeth; for man looketh on the outward appearance, but the Lord looketh on the heart"- 1 Samuel 16:7

I will include a few scriptures that reference the customs (*laws*) required by Jewish men at this time including (*hair, attire, beard, and body.*)

"Doth not even nature itself teach you, that, if a man have long hair, it is a shame unto him?"-1 Corinthians 11:14

"Ye shall not round corners of your heads, neither shalt thou mar the corners of thy beard"-Leviticus 19:27

"For he shall grow up before him as a tender plant, and as a root out of a dry ground: he hath no form nor comeliness; and when we shall see him, there is no beauty that we should desire him."-Isaiah 53:2

"And Jesus saith unto him, the foxes have holes, and the birds of the air have nests; but the Son of Man hath not where to lay his head."- Matthew 8:20, Luke 9:58

As a matter of fact, I was researching this history of Jesus's time and I located a piece of evidence written by a philosopher named Celsus *(2nd Century AD.)* He basically writes about Jesus being (*messy or ratty*) or looking like a *beggar.*

"Jesus wandered about most shamefully in the sight of all" 1:62
"He obtained His means of livelihood on a disgraceful and

importunate way' 1:62 "He was a vagabond...an outcast who roamed about with His body disgracefully unkempt" 2:38

Translations from Henry Chadwick, Origen, Contra Celsum *(Cambridge: Cambridge University Press, 1965).*

> **"His head and his hairs were like white wool, as white as snow; and his eyes were as a flame of fire."-**Revelation 1:14

As you may very well know, this particular description of Jesus was after He was in His glorified form but for the sake of this understanding, His hair was described as *wool*. This could have meant curly hair, but it seems very unlikely that it was long, straight or curly as you may imagine. There are many other ways to come to the conclusion that the image of Jesus wasn't the perfect looking man we envisioned. Jesus was a poor shepherd boy who had only the clothes on His back. He was born in one the smallest cities of *ten* thousand (*Bethlehem*) Jesus's parents were poor, so He was delivered in an animal stable, called a *manger*. Jesus had no reputation or popularity.

> **"But made himself of no reputation, and took upon him the form of a servant, and was made in the likeness of men"-** Philippians 2:7

I've included an original design collaboration of a much more likely version of how Jesus could have looked, (*based upon the geographical locations and conditions of Jesus's day.*) This is obviously not Jesus, but it's based upon the limited details we are given in the Bible. This may not be the image you have ever considered. Remember, Jesus was a Jewish, middle eastern, poor shepherd boy who was not necessarily attractive.

DEAD FRIDAY & RISEN SUNDAY-NOT POSSIBLE!

So this religious myth is interesting! The Bible says that Jesus spent three days and three nights in the tomb right? Well let's take a look at this a little deeper! We see this in Matthew 12, ***"For as Jonas was three days and three nights in the whale's belly; so*** *shall the Son of Man be three days and three nights in the heart of the earth.*"- Matthew 12:40

This clearly shows that Jesus was dead *three* days and *three* nights. Keep in mind that the custom of that day was someone wasn't truly believed to be dead until the fourth day.

> *"Then Jesus came, he found that he had lain in the grave four days already."*-John 11:17

It seems to make a lot of sense to me, considering Jesus told the people that this man's illness wouldn't kill him. Jesus states...

> *"This sickness is not unto death."*- John 11:4

I believe Jesus knew to wait the *four days* in order to gain more spectators, with the possibility of gaining more believers. In this time period, it was widely believed that when someone died, their soul would float around and then re-enter the body. (*I believe*) that Jesus knew this, therefore He waited until the *fourth* day to perform His miracle, with the intent of confirming that Lazarus was truly dead, in order to eliminate the possibility (*in their eyes*) that he wasn't really dead. Jesus knew exactly what He was doing. *We read this, in the book of John...*

> *"Jesus wept."*- John 11:35

This is the shortest sentence in the Bible. (*I believe*) that this is telling the reader something! *God writes everything with a purpose!* This statement can be taken many different ways. *I believe* that Jesus knew it would take something as dramatic as raising a man from the dead, to convince the Jews He was the *"Messiah."* Some scholars believe Jesus uttered these words just as a sign of *fear* and emotion. I believe that Jesus wasn't afraid. I believe Jesus knew the agony of the cross, and He knew when He hung on the cross, He would have no knowledge of God. He knew He would become sin for us. He knew we would reject Him. *This verse expresses the very emotions of Jesus…*

> ***"And about the ninth hour Jesus cried with a loud voice, saying, Eli, Eli, lama sabachthani? that is to say, <u>My God, my God, why hast thou forsaken me?</u>-**Matthew 27:46*

Religious people would say that this is Jesus *(losing his faith)* I would argue that this is Jesus became sin for the world, recorded in the book of Luke. We didn't take His life. ***He Gave It!***

> Luke 19:10 ***"For the Son of man is come to seek and to save that which was lost."**-Matthew 27:46*

Interesting side note: *Jesus makes a very interesting quote that I love…*

> *"And I am glad for your sakes that I was not there, to the intent ye may believers nevertheless let us go unto him."*- John 11:15

Jesus makes the point that if He went one day earlier ***"for their sakes"*** they would not have truly believed that the man came back from the dead! Jesus knew exactly what He was doing, as always! Let's get back to when He actually died and resurrected. On Jesus's day the Jewish calendar started at *sun down* rather than *sun up. ex… 6:01 pm* instead of sun up *ex. 12.01 a.m.* We live in a western world and our days are created according to the Roman calendar. The Bible was written according to a Jewish setting. This set in to motion the Jewish understanding of the day. Their Sabbath started at sun down. You may not have noticed that the Bible says three days and three nights, but if you study all of the passover traditions, you will learn that the year was a High Sabbath and Jesus himself was the *Passover* lamb. Jesus could not have died on Friday and risen on Sunday (*hence Sunday church*) because Friday to Sunday wouldn't make sense when you look at *Matthew 12:40.*

> **"For as Jonas was three days and three nights in the whale's belly; so shall the Son of Man be three days and three nights in the heart of the earth."**- Matthew 12:40

You will realize that the math doesn't add up. After examining the Word, you will soon realize that Jesus would have died on Wednesday after 6pm and rose on Saturday after 6:00 am in the same fashion. *He was The Sabbath." "Do you remember the fifth commandment ? You may notice that during creation, God says "The evening and the morning were the first day, and evening and the morning were the second day and so on. Haven't you ever noticed that creation starts with evening? This is because the Old Testament was written according to the **Jewish Calendar**. Mornings and evenings during that time were opposite of ours. It is the opposite of our Western **Roman calendar**! We call morning, 12:01 A.M. and the Jews called morning 6:01 P.M. This means when the bible says three days and three nights, it would refer to his death after OUR 6:00 P.M. and three days later would be after OUR 6 P.M on Saturday evening! This would be three days and three nights! He IS our Sabbath!*

> **"Remember the Sabbath day, to keep it holy"**- Exodus 20:8 ?

Did it ever occur to you that the commandment mentioned here (*whether it is Saturday or Sunday*) is simply saying...*please just remember Jesus!* He is literally our Sabbath! Or remember *Jesus* and stop all of your religion! This makes a lot more sense, especially when you read the book of Genesis. In Genesis we see the days of creation, and you may have never noticed it is written in this order...

> *"And God called the light Day, and the darkness*
> *he called Night. And the evening and the morning*
> *were called the first day."*-Genesis 1:5

Wait what? Evening and morning? Yes that's right, God wrote the Bible from a Jewish perspective, because this is the time of Jesus! Clearly if it started with evening, we can see the first part of the day was actually evening. But again, our religious assumptions dictate that we are superior to everyone and we always come first. In our own culture, the world revolves around us, it seems. Religion has embedded these thoughts in our head. It's so easy to just hear and adopt whatever was passed down to us through our parents, our church or fundamentally just following the band-wagon. *Please think for yourself!*

EASTER

Easter was a Babylonian practice of worship towards Ishtar, the Golden Egg of Astarte, and associated fertility rites of Spring. <u>Ex</u>-Famous rabbits *(Rabbits that lay Easter Eggs?)* *Think about it!* This is a perfect example of *religion!*

DRAGONS OR DINOSAURS?

> *"In the beginning God created the heaven and the*
> *earth."*-Genesis 1:1

The Bible says for *six* days, the Lord made heaven and earth, the sea. *If all of that in the Bible is true, then Adam would have seen dinosaurs!* Man and dinosaur would have both been around on day six. There are so many different ways that satan used our school systems through the avenue of deceit and lack of understanding, to filter mis-information to our children. The gatekeepers have even twisted our educational textbooks and put out false information. Our English word (*dinosaur*) or (*terrible lizard*), was widely known up until 1841 by Sir Richard Owen. Before this time, dinosaurs were known as *dragons!* That's right, dragons! In the 1891

American Dictionary of the English Language, dinosaurs made their grand entrance. We assume again, because of adopted ideologies that the dinosaur is real and the dragon is fake.

In the 1946 dictionary, the word dragon appears as*"**drag'on.**"* *"**Now rare**.*"*A huge serpent, fabulous animal, generally monstrous winged scaly serpent , lizard, or saurian"Wait what?*

Now rare? It would seem that information changes every year, and I suppose whatever period you were born in, would make the current information available, the most commonly received! It would take someone (*not afraid of criticism and skepticism*) who is interested in learning truth, to research all available information, before their current existence and discover the deeper truths. Just because we are taught something, doesn't mean it's true. People can be very convincing. Some one can put on a nice suit and tie and speak with (*politically correct jargon*) and do it with authority, and we are convinced. This is what we're faced with today. In case you didn't know, *Lizards* and *reptiles*, never stop growing. They must have been very large and terrifying to the people of Adam's time and would eventually be hunted and killed off. Imagine nowadays, if we found a giant bear that was 20 feet tall. I'm willing to bet that eventually we would destroy any bears we found, causing them to be extinct. We see this in our day with any animals that are endangered. The dragon is (*defined by the 1946 dictionary*) which means that these dragons must have been very large and would have become extinct over time for a few obvious reasons.

If you think about it, just *200* years ago, our population was only about *1 billion* people, and now about seven times that. This has only been in *200* years. *Think about it!*

When Jesus was alive, the population was known to be only about ¼ of a billion people alive. Population grows and ferocious animal counts would go down. *This is common sense! This is what happened to dragons!* Dragons are found on the Chinese Zodiac. Dinosaurs are found all over artwork, on walls. Dragons are on the walls in 600 BC. Even Alexandra the Great was reported to have been scared when conquering India in *300 BC,* because of dragons. Roman mosaics show two long necked dragons with their heads together.

The book of Job would have taken place roughly right after the flood and He would have been roughly *300-400* years old.

> *"After this lived Job an hundred and forty years, and saw his sons, and his sons' sons, even four generations."-* Job 42:16

א ת DRAGONS BEHEMOTH LEVIATHAN DINOSAURS ת א

> *"Behold now behemoth, which I made with thee; he eateth grass as an ox."-* In Job 40:15

> *"Canst thou draw out leviathan with an hook? Or his tongue with a cord which thou latest down?"-* In Job 41:1

> *"Who can open the doors of his face? His teeth are terrible round about."-* Job 41:14

> *"Canst thou put an hook into his nose or bore his jaw though with a thorn?"-* Job 41:2

God is asking roughly 80 questions of Job, basically saying these creatures are too big for you to tame! But he is clearly saying these are real animals.

> *"None is fierce that dare stir him up:"-* Job 41:10

Who then is able to stand before me?

205

"His scales are his pride, shut up together with a close seal. One is so near to another, that no air can come between them."- Job 41:15-16

"They are joined one to another, they stick together, that they cannot be sundered."- Job 41:17

"By his <u>neesings</u> a light doth shine, and his eyes are like the eyelids of the morning."- Job 41:18
This word means blowing air out of its nose! Only used here in the bible.

"Out his mouth go burning lamps, and sparks of fire leap out."- Job 41:19

"Out of his nostrils goeth smoke, as out of a seething pot or caldron."- Job 41:20

*"His breath kindleth coals, and a flame goeth out of his mouth."–*Job 41:21

"There went up a smoke out of his nostrils, and fire out of his mouth devoured: coals were kindled by it."- 2 Samuel 22:9

*"And the great dragon was cast out, that old serpent, called the Devil, and Satan, which deceiveth the whole world:"-*Revelation 12:9

Obviously the dragon is symbolic of satan, but there are hundreds of legends about fire breathing dragons. It is possible for Alkali metals such as sodium, potassium and lithium to react with water and produce heat and flammable hydrogen gas, which can ignite or combine explosively with atmospheric oxygen. These are considered *"Water Sensitive Chemicals."* By the way, there are approximately five ways to start a fire only using water. You may be shocked to know that there is an animal that can mix chemicals that sprays from its backside, and burns its enemies, called the *Bombardier Beetle or blister bug. They spray hydrogen peroxide and another hydrogen mixture.* When these two chemicals mix, they heat up to *212* degrees. It fires *500* pulses per second. The same as a rocket mixture.

If evolution were correct and the beetle was transitioning in evolution, then how did this genetic chemical reaction have an in-between stage? It's because God made the beetle its own creation, not an evolutionary creature. *I think I've made my point in these scriptures and scenarios, that evolution is absolutely absurd! Science books change every year, but God's word never changes!*

CLOSING THOUGHTS

I've spent all this time expressing my heart from the beginning of the book. I've promised you my story would be revealed at the end. I've told you that you would have to read it in its entirety to fully understand its purpose.

Jesus said, "*I come in the volume of the book*," and to know Him, is to spend time in His Word. Jesus said that "*the power of life and death is in the tongue*." He said "*not one jot nor tiddle will pass before all laws will be fulfilled.*" Jesus said,**"*I am the Alpha and Omega, the beginning and the end.*"** You won't understand the purpose of the book, unless you've read it entirely, and meditated on its words. *In my opinion*, this message is very clear! *I believe the* reader will receive a deeper understanding of the concealed truth. Anyone who digs into His Word (with a *spiritual radar detector*) or a (*sensitive and discerning spirit*) as well as a deep thirst for the knowledge of God, will receive a blessing. *God has revealed the Bible to us through Jesus Christ!* The Bible has been revealed to the serious readers, who are willing to spend time in it and accept it. ***Jesus is AlephTav***. He is the *strong servant*, who served a destination for you and me. For those who have not taken time to truly get to know the author, they will be confused. God is not the author of confusion, and darkness comprehends, not the light!

To close, _my story is His story_ (**history**) I am simply a voice in the wilderness, hoping to pave the way for even just one person, but it will all be worth it. So let's join together in faith and celebrate the **life, death** and **resurrection** of our Lord and Savior, **Jesus Christ**! To all believers on Jesus Christ, _We are The 70_!

> **"After these things the Lord appointed other seventy also, and sent them two and two before his face into every city and place, whither he himself would come."**- Luke 10:1

"We are the Remnant."

> **"And I will gather the remnant of my flock out of all countries whither I have driven them, and will bring them again to their folds; and they shall be fruitful and increase."**- Jeremiah 23:3

We are the faithful servants, the salt of the earth and the strongman of the remnant!

> **"Ye are the salt of the earth: but if the salt have lost his savour, wherewith shall it be salted? it is thenceforth good for nothing, but to be cast out, and to be trodden under foot of men."**-Matthew 5:13

God is long suffering in His attempt at getting our attention, even right before the rapture in Revelation 4:1. Remember these words if you've heard nothing else I've said up until now!

> **"He that hath an ear, let him hear what the Spirit saith unto the churches."**- Revelation 3:22

> **"My heart is inditing a good matter: I speak of the things which I have made touching the king: my tongue is the pen of a ready writer."**- Psalms 45:1

"And he said unto them, Go ye into all the world, and preach the gospel to every creature."-
Mark 16:16

Please share this book with the world. I love you and God loves you more!

AMEN

TO CONCLUDE

"free yourself from religion"

Seek out truth, through the Word of God, not the words of men!

"The thief cometh not, but for to steal, and to kill, and to destroy: I am come that they might have life, and that they might have it more abundantly."- John 10:10

MY TESTIMONY

> *"For where your <u>treasure</u> is, there will your heart be also."*

KJV- Matthew 6:21

This scripture *"still"* echoes in my ears today! It was *May 14, 2015*. I had the world in my hands. I was self-employed with multiple business locations, making more money than I knew what to do with. I might have said I was living large! I felt powerful! I had money and a wife who worked beside me. I had three kids, who spent most of their lives moving from house to house, through all of my mess. (*One of which was an employee of mine, who would, eventually take over our family business.*) I felt socially popular, accepted and if you would have asked me, I would have told you that I was a good person! *Wrong* It wasn't until I read *Mark 10:18,"**And Jesus said unto him, Why callest thou me good?"** "There is none good but one, that is, God."*

> **"As it is written, there is none righteous, no, not one:"** Matthew 3:10

I was *39* years old. Life was good! My favorite thing to do was complain about everything and blame everyone for my failures. I was full of pride. I thought the world revolved around me. I had no comprehension of how good my life was. Most of my life I wasn't even an honest person *(even to myself.)* I had moved out at the young age of *thirteen*, living in basements, all around the city of Newton, Iowa. I spent most of my nights at (*Taylor's basement.*) *(Good old Charlie.) Charlie was our friend, (Aaron's) dad. This guy was the nicest dude you've ever met! He let us all party all night and drink until we passed out!* At the time, that made him cool in my eyes! *To this day I'll still never know how we all survived the craziness of it all!* I couldn't stand people rattling on about God and the Bible. I'll never forget my grandma. This woman would go on and on about God! I wasn't a big fan of hers, because I always felt judged by her. Just a few years ago *(after getting to know Jesus)* I had a chance to see my grandma again, just before she passed away. I took her to get her nails done, and as I pushed her in a wheelchair. I really enjoyed her company that whole day. Looking back now, I've realized that I was partly at fault, and her faith was upsetting my spirit. I can't leave out my Dad. This man literally made me crazy! I hated him so many times, for so many different reasons until God took control of my life. This is what happened. I realized that there was no instruction manual in life. He was in my boat, and it hit me that all of my independent, tough love lessons that I'd taught my son, I got from him. The second half of my life, I have to thank my former in-laws, *(Wally & LaNell)* had their own mess *(just like all of us)* but they taught me finances, and let me tell you, in my wildest dreams I'd never expected the life that would follow...

Fast forward to 6 years ago, on the morning of *May 14, 2015*. I was awakened early by my son, who has never been one to show much emotion. He was yelling and crying and said,*"Dad, I think I killed my sisters!"* All I could think about was the desperation in his voice, *(like I've never heard before.)* He called me early, while driving his sisters to school around *8 a.m.* in the morning. He must have been rushing to take his sisters to school. (*With very little sleep the night before.*) I'm sure he was already frustrated as well as sleepy at that point. I'm not sure how my brain processed all of it, but somehow it did. I immediately grabbed my keys and rushed down the country road, I assumed he would have taken.

There was no way I could have prepared for what I saw! As I pulled up to the scene, I jumped out of the car, and it was still in motion. I had no idea that my entire life would change in about thirty minutes. My son's car was upside down in the ditch. The impact knocked over a light pole and sent a tree into someone's front yard. All I could see in the distance were ambulances, fire trucks, police officers and paramedics scurrying in all directions. *I was in absolute shock!* I felt like I was standing all alone on top of the world's highest mountain. There was chaos, and people yelling all around me, but I could only see their lips moving. *I just shut down mentally. This was the day that I thought that everything I loved was gone! Forever!* I had never really talked with God *(seriously)* before that day. I saw my son, *(face down,)* yelling at the paramedics, *"leave me alone!,"* *"help my sisters!"*

I fell to my knees! On my left was my oldest daughter, with two black eyes, bleeding, and the swelling was already beginning to protrude from her forehead. On my right, was my youngest daughter, her long blond hair stained red from blood dripping out of her mouth. As the gurney braces were being placed on both sides of her face, I placed my head on my son's chest. I was holding each one of my daughters hands, and I prayed boldly for God's help!

This is where my journey began. *I cried my eyes out and begged God to save my children!* Jesus became the Lord of my life and I vowed to serve Him, not just as a believer, but as a minister of the gospel. I'd taken my promise to God very seriously, and I knew He was listening! Here's the thing, I had no idea what that meant. I hated reading, public speaking, and I definitely had no plans of lifting my hands in public! I pleaded for God to heal my kids. I remember begging God to help me and I swore that I would serve Him forever. The very moment I agreed to minister the Gospel I heard, *"Ok, get up, they're going home!"* I got up and looked to my right as my oldest daughter was being loaded into the ambulance and she said to me, *"Dad, am I dying?"* At that time, I didn't realize the *Holy Spirit* was speaking to me, and I responded, *"baby, would I ever lie to you about something this important?, "no dad,"* she responded." I told her, *"Baby you're going home tonight, I promise!" I just heard God's voice, and He told me you were going home tonight!"* She looked directly in my eyes and replied, *"I believe you...dad."* Later at the hospital, the chaplain and doctors were assuring me that I was in shock, but I kept telling them, *"I'm **not** in shock," They're going home tonight! I heard it from God!* The doctor came out and said, *"We have run every test imaginable and besides some cuts, scrapes and a fractured rib. They are leaving tonight!"* I asked *"What are the odds of a vehicle flying upside down and wrapping into a pole, and someone surviving such a crash?"* and the doctor said, *"Zero"*.

From that day, I never looked back and would go on to get a ministry license and become a pastor. The rest is history! *My point is that God can use the smallest of people to do the biggest of things*! A few months went by and I gave up my tattoo business. I passed by a little church in the country one day and decided I would go check it out. I was sitting in the pews and the preacher was discussing the book of Timothy.

> ***"For the love of money is the root of all evil:"*** - 1
> Timothy 6:10

The pastor walked right up to me, and said, ***"For where your treasure is, there will your heart be also."*** Matthew 6:21

I was blown away!

I looked down at myself sitting there, and it occurred to me that I had spent my whole life obsessed with myself. I realized that my treasure was my *"stuff."* This *completely* rocked my world, right after almost losing all three of my children. I ended up handing my tattoo shop to my son (*who continues to build a successful business*) where I left off. I had no passion or purpose for anything else after that point. I took a job as a property manager and a prison officer at the same time to make ends meet. I knew exactly what my true purpose was! My **treasure** became *Jesus Christ!* As my walk with Jesus progressed, I spent time in church all around the city. I realized I was in search of truth, but every church I visited had so many religious opinions of Jesus. I figured I'd better find out quickly, who this *Jesus* really was. Eventually, I was recommended to a church called *Word of God Ministries.* The Pastor was jumping up and down and yelling, but in a good way. *This man got me excited about serving God!* He kept saying *"Jesus is the Manifested Word of God,"* and quoting...

> **"In the beginning was the Word, and the Word was with God, and the Word was God."**-John 1:1

I realized the only thing I needed to know was *"who is Jesus?"*

This began my journey to find truth, and avoid religion all together. Of course the first step for me, was determining which version of the Bible to read, and why. I've been so apprehensive about reading commentaries or literature that may lead me down the wrong path. *I don't want to be influenced or convinced by a man, or a church or a religious tradition! I don't want to be taught lies or myths! I want to be led by God alone!* I'm not here to defend the Bible or even promote the Bible. I am here to do exactly what John the Baptist did, in *John 1:23.* He said...

> **"I am the voice of one crying in the wilderness, make straight the way of the Lord, as said by the prophet Esaias."**- John 1:23

I heard a man once say that *"The Bible doesn't need defending because it is like a wild lion in a cage. Once you open it, it will defend itself."*

First we need to read from the true Word of God!

"But thou, O Daniel, shut up the words, and seal the book, even to the time of the end: many shall run to and fro, and knowledge shall be increased."-

Daniel 2:4

Amen

MEET THE AUTHOR

John G. Smith ll, *"Preacher Man,"* by his friends, is the founding pastor of *"The Little Word Church,"* in Shreveport, Louisiana. His heart dramatically changed May 14th, 2015, when his three children were involved in a traumatic accident. He felt called to the ministry from that point forward. He has since spent the last five years developing an *(online Christian Digital Library.)* Pastor John is known for his *off the wall*, and *"quirky"* personality and his passion for teaching the Gospel of Jesus!

<u>Contact info:</u>
Pastor John G. Smith ll
The Little Word Church
www.thelittlewordchurch.com
thelittlewordchurch@youtube.com
www.thelittlewordchurch@gmail.com
www.rockirons@gmail.com

JESUS *IS* THE REVELATION

Revelation 1:1 *"The Revelation of Jesus Christ" (**not** the revelation of the antichrist*.) Religion is satan's method of destruction! He knows, but will always twist the Word of God with lies, tradition and religion. God's Word *is* Truth. Too often we *listen to the Gatekeepers and adopt their belief systems!* Lies have taught our children that explosions create, rather than destroy! The enemy wants death to look good and wants us to choose *him*, over God. You cannot separate God's Spirit from His Word!

B*lack cats, 666, and the #13 are man-made fears*! The King James Bible is God's perfect, inspired, and preserved words. If He can preserve His Words for over *1500* years, then why couldn't He have done it perfectly! God used the hands of over 40 authors and placed Himself within the volume of His literal (*God breathed*) Hebrew *letters.* Hosea 4:6 says, "*My people are destroyed for lack of knowledge.*" We will explore scripture, charts and Hebrew messages. Let's look for (*Jesus) Christ* rather than "*antichrist.*" Jesus is on *every single page*! Let's take an exciting journey that will open our eyes in an exciting new way!

ת א FINAL PRAYER ת א

Father God thank you for Your Word

Thank you for leading us through the avenue of Your Holy Spirit
Father I acknowledge that Your Word alone is Truth
And there is no Truth, but through Your Son, Jesus Christ
I pray that all who are lost and bound by religion
Will hear Your voice, and it will convict them
Thank you for being Lord of our lives
And for leading us into salvation
Your Word says
According to John 1:1
That in the beginning
You were the Aleph Tav
The Alpha and Omega
Who was the Word
Who was with God
And who was God
You are the lamb Who opened the seal of Revelation 6
You are the 5th horseman of Revelation 19
Who gave His life for us
So that we might know You God
Father I ask that You would use my tongue
To speak Your Word
And advance Your kingdom
In the earth, as in heaven
That my life would glorify You
In thanksgiving praise and worship
Father Your Word says that
We have been redeemed
satan is overcome
We are victorious

And Jesus is Lord

In Jesus name

Amen

"Jesus saith unto him, I am the way, the truth, and the life: no man cometh unto the Father, but by me."- John 14:6

א ת

CPSIA information can be obtained
at www.ICGtesting.com
Printed in the USA
LVHW061219220421
684915LV00002BA/128

9 781662 813214